THE COURAGE
TO GROW

THE COURAGE TO GROW

LEADING WITH INTENTIONALITY

Kristine Servais and Kellie Sanders

ROWMAN & LITTLEFIELD PUBLISHERS, INC.
Lanham • Boulder • New York • Toronto • Plymouth, UK

Published by Rowman & Littlefield Publishers, Inc.
A wholly owned subsidiary of
The Rowman & Littlefield Publishing Group, Inc.
4501 Forbes Boulevard, Suite 200, Lanham, Maryland 20706
http://www.rowmanlittlefield.com

10 Thornbury Road, Plymouth PL6 7PP, United Kingdom

British Library Cataloguing in Publication Information Available

Library of Congress Cataloging-in-Publication Data

Servais, Kristine, 1954–
  The courage to grow : leading with intentionality / Kristine Servais and
Kellie Sanders.
      p. cm.
  Includes bibliographical references and index.
  ISBN 978-1-4422-1607-5 (cloth : alk. paper) — ISBN 978-1-4422-1601-3
(pbk. : alk. paper) — ISBN 978-1-4422-1602-0 (electronic)
  1. School management and organization—Handbooks, manuals, etc.
  2. Educational leadership—Handbooks, manuals, etc. I. Sanders, Kellie,
1967– II. Title.
  LB2805.S5414 2012
  371.2–dc23
                                                    2011045109

Printed in the United States of America

CONTENTS

CONTENTS

ACKNOWLEDGMENTS

First and foremost, we are grateful for the many lessons we have learned from our students. We are also thankful for the many people in our lives that contributed to *The Courage to Grow: Leading with Intentionality*. First, we thank our parents, our first teachers, who modeled courage and the desire for us to grow every day as we were growing up. We appreciate the professional relationships with leaders such as Douglas Reeves and Elle Allison, who took the time and interest to provide us with feedback on this book.

A special thanks to the following friends and colleagues who were willing to read, edit, read, and edit as many times as necessary to prepare this manuscript for publication: Mary Lynne Derrington, John Harper, Linell Monson-Laswell, Don McKinney, William Shields, and our gifted editor Donna Davis.

Finally, we are grateful to our life coaches, Carol and Jenni, for their endless patience and moxie during our constant leadership growth.

INTRODUCTION

Getting Ready for the Courage to Grow

People driven by intention are described as having a strong will that won't permit anything to interfere with achieving their inner desire.

—Wayne Dyer, 2004, p. 3

The Courage to Grow: Leading with Intentionality will show educational leaders how to design and carry out a personal professional development/learning plan. It is a guide that allows leaders to construct their own learning to measure knowledge, assess growth, and improve performance. For our purposes, "intentionality" is defined as an intense energy or desire to grow exponentially from our current reality.

> Intention is not groggy in the morning. The day is met with a particular enthusiasm. The possibilities of the day are partners—not adversaries. Intentional living recognizes that, while accidents happen, life is not an accident. Days are built choice by choice. Intention savors moments of peaceful contemplation equally with productive initiative. Intention knows each moment of the day as a precious moment. (Radmacher, 2007, p. 21)

Why *The Courage to Grow*? This training manual is for the teacher leader, beginning principal, practicing principal, assistant principal, department chair, district office administrator, aspiring leadership candidate, and college preparation program professor. Research is clear on the vital role of the principal for student achievement (Marzano,

Waters, & McNulty, 2005). Even more compelling is the research on the importance of effective leadership in high-need schools (Lyman & Villani, 2004). However, state and national reports on progress being made in the preparation of successful school leaders continue to be bleak and alarming. Effective leadership does not happen randomly or by accident. It is conducted with a high level of intention that what is desired can be accomplished. *The Courage to Grow: Leading with Intentionality* is a guide for leaders at all levels to take action.

The Courage to Grow is a follow-up to *The Courage to Lead: Choosing the Road Less Traveled*, a workbook of ten essential skills and practical resources for collaborative leaders. Both of these resources are based on the premise that our greatest learning occurs through a commitment to action. Douglas Reeves (2004a) provides leaders with many motives to take informed and evaluative action, including research on the knowing-doing gap, which suggests that leaders frequently possess the knowledge to take action but fail to do so. Successful leaders take action that is congruent with knowledge in the best interest of students and the organization while continuously striving to self-assess, grow, and improve.

The Courage to Grow will allow leaders to complete a leadership *fitness* assessment in chapters 2–7. Interstate School Leaders Licensure Consortium (ISLLC) performance standards (Council of Chief State School Officers, 2008) are used for the assessment as a practical tool for measuring present and future leadership skills. Each chapter provides ways to improve leadership skills and assess your own performance for the role you currently fulfill (district office, school administrator, leadership candidate/teacher leader, or educational leadership professor). The chapters are designed to address the comprehensive nature of the school leader. Thomas Sergiovanni (2009) compares the functions of a competent leader to the images of the head, heart, and hands. The multifaceted levels of the ISLLC 2008 performance standards are used within this text to illustrate the head as knowledge, heart as dispositions, and hands as performance. Chapters begin with a section called "Learning with Intentionality," followed by a personal application of "Caring with Intentionality." Chapters 2–7 will have a section titled "Assessing with Intentionality" and conclude with "Growing with Intentionality," which requires the balanced application of leadership. Depending on your leadership role, you can select activities best suited to increase performance from present realities to ideal conditions for learning. Readers are encouraged to design personal action plans that take into account knowledge from each chapter, strategies for increasing their performance with intentionality, and self-assessment results. Finally, each chapter includes websites, resources, and activities to improve leadership.

Successful athletes and school leaders share many of the same characteristics. Athletes are acutely aware of their present level of fitness, goal setting, improvement of skills, and performance expectations. Similarly, leaders must be conscious of their own goals, improvement, and performance. However, in the field of education, understanding the need for leadership growth and improvement of performance is rare (Reeves, 2004a). Equally rare are tools or resources for leaders to assess their own growth and development, and well-defined performance expectations are ambiguous. Imagine that as an athlete you have prepared and trained for a golf tournament, and upon arrival to the event you find that the event is actually a marathon and you are expected to run 26.2 miles. The element of surprise and inadequate preparation is a common scenario for many school leaders. Leaders need to be aware of leadership expectations and the skills needed to be successful.

The Courage to Grow is a training guide much like one used to improve physical fitness. Comparisons are made between leadership development and fitness-based activities. Similar characteristics between leadership and fitness include goal setting, commitment, self-assessment, and teaming for success. Readers are encouraged to measure their own *leadership fitness* level and discover methods to improve, assess, and perform in a variety of settings in which they lead.

Imagine a modern-day Rip Van Winkle waking up a decade from now and visiting a school. Would he find that little has changed while he was sleeping, or would he find remarkably positive changes? Ideally, he would find the school community highly engaged with many partners, including parents, college professors, teachers, and school leaders. He would also observe a school where learning is central in regard to time, resources, and decisions. Leadership is collective and collaborative, as many are empowered with the responsibility to make decisions and contributions toward their shared commitments. The educational leadership professor and the principal work concurrently to develop authentic leadership opportunities in the school that will positively impact student achievement. Problem solving is no longer done in a vacuum but rather collaboratively as all stakeholders take action as student advocates. Learning is at the center of all decisions and is integrated into the mission and purpose of the school community. Throughout this book you will see the potential for new roles and greater impact by the superintendent, professor, school administrator, teacher leader, parents, and students. Most noteworthy is that what was once the ideal can become the reality. There is a critical need for leaders to set and achieve a vision for the ideal conditions of a learning environment.

The Hope Foundation and fourteen top leaders in our country recommended to President Barack Obama that, to ensure the development of twenty-first-century school leaders, leadership should be focused on a combination of student learning, progress, and culture building, while enhancing the quality of teaching. *The Courage to Grow: Leading with Intentionality* takes leaders one step closer to meeting this comprehensive recommendation and provides knowledge and strategies that transform leaders from a focus on present realities to the ideals possible for all learners. The ability to inspire others to reach for a dream is nothing new to successful leadership. As Lance Secretan (2004) said, when referring to leadership, "You will learn the process that will reveal the real purpose of your life, why you are here, what you are meant to do while you are here, how you will do it, how you will serve, how you can invite others to fully participate with you, and how you can inspire them and therefore yourself" (p. xxvii). In other words, leaders must be able to understand themselves deeply in order to lead effectively.

This introduction, "Getting Ready for the Courage to Grow," sets the reader up for the learning experiences that will occur throughout the book. Chapter 1 explains why leading with intentionality is important and that leadership assessment should drive improvement for the entire learning community. Chapters 2–7 utilize the Educational Leadership Policy Standards: ISLLC 2008 to provide a framework for what leaders should know and be able to do. Within these chapters, you find leadership dispositions: "Dispositions have been influential in emphasizing the underlying assumptions, values, and beliefs appropriate to an education system that is dedicated to high expectations for each and every student. Effective leaders analyze their assumptions, values, and beliefs as part of reflective practice" (Council of Chief State School Officers, 2008, p. 6). Dispositions are used as subheadings in these chapters to help you learn how to strengthen your leadership attitudes and beliefs. Chapter 8 provides the reader with a wide range of engaged learning processes (ELPs), which are designed to assist the leader in providing impactful staff development. Chapter 9 wraps up *The Courage to Grow* by allowing you, the reader, to celebrate your growth throughout the text as well as learn about personal and organizational celebration ideas.

The Courage to Grow should not be completed alone. It is meant to be interactive with peers, teacher leaders, and professors of leadership at all levels of learning. For example, a superintendent can utilize *The Courage to Grow* to determine activities that the district administrative team can complete together. The chapters provide interactive learning processes and activities designed to encourage leaders from different levels to practice and improve competencies for each standard. As such, these activities require a high element of risk taking. While our instincts tell us it is safer to continue to support the status quo, we know that keeping things the same only increases the knowing-doing gap. In other words, the temptation is to learn but not apply what we have learned. The reader of *The Courage to Grow: Leading with Intentionality* will not grow without taking a degree of intentional risk and action. This can be compared to the growth and development of a lobster. We use a lobster as a metaphor for risk taking because lobsters can only grow physically if they take risks within their environment. Lobsters can only grow to the size of their outer shells. In order to grow larger, they must crack their shells and become vulnerable to their surroundings—only then will they re-grow new shells. Lobsters will go through many risk-taking cycles throughout their lives as they continue to crack open their shells, grow larger, re-grow their shells, and so on. We encourage you, the reader, to be lobster-like as you grow.

At the conclusion of this book, you will walk away with a personal leadership fitness plan that utilizes baseline data of your individual competencies, followed by application and reassessment of growth. A leadership growth plan is only a start. It will be imperative to intentionally put the plan into action in order to grow and develop as a leader.

Successful leaders are able to engage and collaborate with others. One thing to strongly consider before beginning this growth journey is finding a colleague or group of leaders with whom to work collaboratively. Administrators in today's schools are utilizing a shared leadership model that enables them to collaborate much more effectively than in the past. Educational leaders are most effective when leadership is collaborative, collective, and compassionate (Raelin, 2003). Use *The Courage to Grow* as a book study that can assist all of you in growing into the outstanding leaders you are meant to be. It is not a role for the faint of heart. But it is a heartfelt role that will change you and your world. It is complex and simple at the same time. So, "[l]ive with intention, walk to the edge, listen hard, practice wellness, laugh, risk, continue to learn, appreciate your friends, choose no regret, fail with enthusiasm, lead or follow a leader, do what you love, and live as if this is all there is" (Radmacher, 2007, p. 20).

1

LEADERSHIP GROWTH

Knowing the Objectives of the Game

The greater danger for most of us is not that our aim is too high and we miss it, but that it is too low and we reach it.

—Michelangelo

 LEARNING WITH INTENTIONALITY

Why Leadership Assessment?

Leadership assessment is essential to the growth and development of competent leaders. Reform is needed to align new models of educational leadership with effective methods of assessment: "If leadership evaluation is to be used constructively, then those conducting the evaluation must never be content merely to render a judgment" (Reeves, 2004a, p. 57). A meaningful evaluation process is needed for future and practicing leaders. It is the obligation of district leadership to formalize an evaluation process for administrators to assist them in their individual performance and growth.

Douglas Reeves suggests that leadership assessment should not be one-dimensional if it is meant to enhance a leader's growth and development: "[Multidimensional leadership assessment] will force school systems to establish clear, coherent, and fair expectations for present and future leaders" (Reeves, 2004a, p. 9). Imagine trying to play lacrosse without knowing the objectives of the game, what equipment is used, and how to score. It is unlikely that we could be successful participants without this information. Often, school leaders find themselves in this same predicament. Although school leaders desire to be successful, they may not be equipped or properly prepared with the knowledge and skills to successfully perform the role expected of them.

Key Elements of Leadership Assessment

Leaders need to have the skills and abilities to self-assess in order to determine the areas in which they need to grow and improve. The primary purpose of leadership self-assessment is to promote the growth and development of those who are being evaluated (Weaver-Hart, 1994; Marcoux, Brown, Irby, & Lara-Alecio, 2003). When leaders are aware of their strengths and weaknesses, ultimately this knowledge will lead to actions that support their individual growth and development (Alimo-Metcalfe, 1998). However, leaders typically experience changing performance expectations, and this makes it difficult for them to know whether they are performing at a competent level.

Leadership evaluation should be aligned with clearly defined job responsibilities and the competencies that the district desires. Evaluation is defined by Ben Harris and Betty Jo Monk (1992) as "a three-phase process involving (a) determination of the competencies desired, (b) description of performance in terms of desired competencies, and (c) making of judgments or decisions based on the closeness of fit between the desired and described competencies" (p. 151). Leadership evaluation is seen by many as being ambiguous and arbitrary, making it almost impossible for a leader to identify areas of growth and development within their position (Reeves, 2004a). It is critical for leaders to understand leadership evaluation practices and its impact on student achievement and teacher success.

The meta-analysis conducted by Robert Marzano, Timothy Waters, and Brian McNulty (2005) determined that increases in student achievement are linked to successful school leadership. Improving student achievement is at the forefront of the educational arena due in part to the federal policies related to the reauthorization of the Elementary and Secondary Education Act (ESEA) of 2001, commonly referred to as No Child Left Behind (NCLB): "The passage of No Child Left Behind has generated new thinking about the role of principal evaluation in boosting individual and organizational performance" (Lashway, 2003, p. 1). Leadership evaluations have been developed with an emphasis on leadership skills determined to improve instruction as well as shape the culture, vision, and values of the school (Lepard, 2002). Researchers have found that principals do make a difference in student learning, but they do so indirectly by influencing internal processes. These internal processes include setting educational expectations, establishing a school vision, and supervising curriculum delivery (Davis, 1998). Imagine the difference principals could make if they were effectively evaluated to improve performance.

Mark Anderson (1991) suggests nine steps that school systems should use to measure effective leadership within the district's organizational structure. These steps include identification of the evaluation's purpose, development of comprehensible performance expectations, collaborative planning with the principal, encouragement of goal setting and reflective practice, direct observation, feedback from stakeholders, artifact collection, taking a cyclical approach to evaluation, and rewarding exceptional performance (as cited in Thomas, Holdaway, & Ward, 2000). These practices in conjunction create a comprehensive model that encompasses all aspects of leadership growth and development, consequently improving performance over time.

Improving leadership performance begins with clear expectations and measurable goals. The use of SMART goals is suggested as a means to set achievable and measurable goals. The term SMART is used to describe goals that are *specific, measurable, attainable, results oriented,* and *time bound* (DuFour, DuFour, Eaker, & Many, 2006). Supervisors are encouraged to guide leaders in setting a limited number of goals, constructing these as SMART goals, and reviewing progress on an ongoing basis. When we write goals using the following formula, we are more likely to achieve them:

We will improve _____ [specific and measurable item] by _____ [what strategies will be used to succeed] by _____ [when]. We will assess our success by _____ [what type of measurement will be used].

CARING WITH INTENTIONALITY

Reflective Practice

Reflective practice is a critical component of leadership improvement. It may be used as an informal or a formal component of the leadership evaluation process. Leaders need to model the desire to grow and improve their leadership competencies. They should have an awareness of their individual strengths and be able to continually assess areas of weakness in order to grow as a leader. It has been stated, "If we are trying to foster the concept that children should be continuous learners, and teachers should continually strive to improve their performance by becoming critical self-appraisers, then principals should model this behavior and be continuous learners as well" (Thomas, Holdaway, & Ward, 2000, p. 227).

Reflective practice is a skill that like other skills must be taught and practiced with colleagues: "Reflection may be an especially important learning process in educational organizations because of the changing social and political demands on these institutions. The awareness of this need is evident by the fact that many preparation programs for school administrators have been prominent advocates of reflection as an instructional methodology for preparing principals and other educational administrators" (White, Crooks, & Melton, 2002, p. 46). A popular and practical resource available for reflective practice for individuals, teams, and schools is *Reflective Practice to Improve Schools: An Action Guide for Educators* (York-Barr, Sommers, Ghere, & Montie, 2001). This resource provides ways to practice and apply reflection that directly impact leading and learning.

A Model for Effective Leadership Assessment

Figure 1.1 (appearing toward the end of this chapter) displays the concepts of leadership evaluation presented in this chapter in one integrated model. This leadership evaluation model was developed as a result of the dissertation titled "The Purpose and Practices of Leadership Assessment as Perceived by Select Public Middle and Elementary School Principals in the Midwest" (Sanders, 2008). Sanders's model was created as a multidimensional leadership evaluation that allows the school or district leader to reflect, analyze various data sources, continuously dialogue with peers as well as evaluators, and create and implement goals in order to impact student achievement.

 ## GROWING WITH INTENTIONALITY: LEADERSHIP GROWTH

All leaders should look for action opportunities to strengthen their growth and development. It isn't enough for leaders to know what they need to do to improve their skills; they need to take action toward desired goals. In this section you find activities for all levels of leadership. The term "leadership candidate" is used to describe educators who are currently pursuing a degree in educational leadership. Teacher leaders are those who have taken on leadership responsibilities within their school or district with or without a leadership endorsement. Activities that you can participate in to strengthen your leadership are listed in the following section.

District- and School-Level Administrator

- Complete the leadership self-evaluations found in chapters 2–7, and determine activities within your work environment that will improve areas of weakness.
- Stay current on leadership research, theory, and best practices by reading professional periodicals and texts. Develop a book talk with your colleagues on a favorite leadership resource.
- Conduct surveys of students, parents, teachers, support staff, community members, district office personnel, and so forth, in order to obtain knowledge of their expectations and needs. Once these surveys are compiled, create a plan of action to address these stakeholders' expectations and needs.
- Meet with leadership colleagues on a continual basis to share thoughts, goals, and ideas on how to grow and develop leadership skills and abilities. Consider sharing your leadership self-evaluations with each other as a means of reflective practice and collegial support.

CHAPTER 1

Educational Leadership Professor

- Complete the leadership self-evaluations found in chapters 2–7, and determine your personal leadership strengths and challenges.
- Review and analyze current leadership research, theory, and best practices by attending conferences, participating in web-based leadership discussions and workshops, and reading periodicals and texts. Incorporate current findings into classroom discussions and activities.
- Attend and participate in state-level meetings to stay current on educational leadership standards and practices in order to enhance not only your personal leadership competencies but also your instructional delivery to future leaders.
- Stay involved and active in local schools and districts to remain current in your knowledge of leadership evaluation practices.

Leadership Candidate and Teacher Leader

- Complete the leadership self-evaluation found in chapters 2–7, and determine areas of strength and areas of need. Understand that, because of your current role, you may not have experience in many of the indicators.
- Review your past evaluations to determine your areas for growth. By reflecting on past performance, it will be easier for you to plan future opportunities and areas of professional development. Establish SMART goals, described in this chapter, to reach your desired outcomes.
- Survey parents, students, and colleagues to determine areas for growth. Establish SMART goals to reach your desired outcomes.
- Take time to meet with your current administrators or mentor to allow them to share their insights into your leadership competencies. By scheduling ongoing meetings with these individuals, you will gain knowledge and strategies to improve your leadership within the classroom and beyond.

INDIVIDUAL LEADERSHIP ACTION PLAN

In each chapter you are asked to create an individual leadership action plan for yourself based on the knowledge and activities you have learned about. Review the "Growing with Intentionality" section, and determine goals that you will establish.

As a result of reading this chapter, I will take the following actions:

I will improve _____ [specific and measurable item] by _____ [what strategies will be used to succeed] by _____ [when]. I will assess my growth by _____ [what type of measurement will be used].

I will improve _____ [specific and measurable item] by _____ [what strategies will be used to succeed] by _____ [when]. I will assess my growth by _____ [what type of measurement will be used].

Figure 1.1. Multidimensional Leadership Evaluation: A Theoretical Model

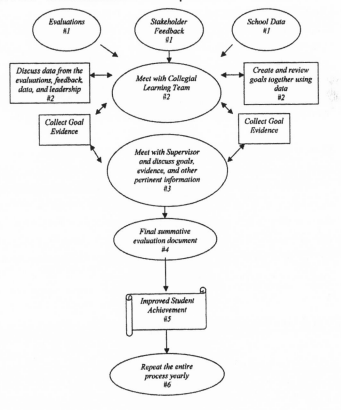

1. Administrators collect multiple pieces of feedback from peers and supervisors, and complete self-evaluations of their leadership competencies. Simultaneously, administrators collect their school or district academic, cultural, and community data in order to share with their colleagues. Data should include stakeholder feedback collected during the prior year.

2. The administrator meets with several colleagues in similar positions to discuss self-evaluations as well as school or district data to determine appropriate individual leadership goals that they will set for themselves for the upcoming year. This learning team approach to goal setting allows for conversational reflection on the information they are sharing. Teams should meet several times throughout the year for collegial conversation about the goals they are individually working toward and make adjustments as necessary.

3. Once the initial goals have been established, with the assistance of the learning team, administrators meet with their district-level supervisors to share goals and, if necessary, make adjustments. Step 3 of this theoretical leadership evaluation model allows for continuous conversational reflection that should occur throughout the year. The principals continue to meet with their supervisors and learning teams, and collect evidence of goal attainment as a cyclical process throughout the school year.

4. The fourth step of the theoretical multidimensional leadership evaluation model is the final summative evaluation document. The supervisors along with the administrator meet to discuss the multiple pieces of evaluation evidence and documentation that have been reviewed and collected throughout the year. From this information, a summative evaluation document is created and shared with each administrator and provides substantive suggestions for leadership improvement and sustainability.

5. The critical final step of this theoretical model is a comprehensive multidimensional evaluation process, supported within a district, which ultimately leads to improved student achievement.

The process begins again the next year, following the same procedures.

LEADERSHIP TOOLS AND RESOURCES FOR GROWTH

360-degree educational impact assessments:
www.educationalimpact.com/360

Vanderbilt assessment of leadership in education:
www.thinklinkassessment.com/corporate/valed.html

Wallace Foundation with a focus on educational leadership:
www.wallacefoundation.org

Leadership and Learning Center:
www.leadandlearn.com

2

A LEADER'S VISION

Making Our Dreams a Reality

A magnificent vision articulates people's hopes and dreams, touches their hearts and spirits, and helps them see how they can contribute. It aims everyone in the right direction.

—Blanchard, 2010, p. 30

ISLLC STANDARD 1

Education leaders ensure the achievement of all students by guiding the development and implementation of a shared vision of learning, strong organizational mission, and high expectations for every student.

Standard 1 Summary

Education leaders are accountable and have unique responsibilities for developing and implementing a vision of learning to guide organizational decisions and actions. Education leaders guide a process for developing and revising a shared vision, strong mission, and goals that are high and achievable for every student when provided with appropriate, effective learning opportunities.

The vision, mission, and goals represent what the community intends for students to achieve, informed by the broader social and policy environment and including policy requirements about specific outcomes and continuous improvement. The vision, mission, and goals become the touchstone for decisions, strategic planning, and change processes. They are regularly reviewed and adjusted, using varied sources of information and ongoing data analysis.

Leaders engage the community to reach consensus about vision, mission, and goals. To be effective, processes of establishing vision, mission, and goals should incorporate diverse perspectives in the broader school community and create consensus to which all can commit. While leaders engage others in developing and implementing the vision, mission, and goals, it is undeniably their responsibility to advocate for and act to increase equity and social justice. (Council of Chief State School Officers, 2008, p. 13)

 LEARNING WITH INTENTIONALITY

Among the dreams, hopes, and ideals of effective leaders is a vision. A vision is a constant reaching for ideals without accepting complacency as the norm. Often, leaders and stakeholders within an organization accept complacency within their school systems because they haven't dreamed big enough to imagine a system even greater than their current reality. Stakeholders may give a multitude of reasons for this complacency, but in the end these are just excuses for sustaining the status quo. "In fewer than 10 percent of the organizations we have visited were members clear about the vision. This lack of shared vision causes people to become inundated with multiple priorities, duplication of efforts, false starts, and wasted energy" (Blanchard, 2010, p. 18). In order for schools and districts to strive for excellence, they must work collaboratively to create, implement, and steward a large-scale vision. A vision is a mental map of the astounding potential for the future of an organization. The leader collaboratively creates and communicates the vision that shapes educational programs, plans, and actions to ensure student success.

The vision of a school or district should incorporate the beliefs, commitments, and dreams of the entire community: "The vision serves as a clear and agreed-upon visual depiction of the promises and commitments the members make to themselves and the organization" (Servais & Sanders, 2006, p. 30). Leaders often confuse "vision" and "mission," but in simple terms, the vision of the organization is the ideal for the future, and the mission is what daily actions we will take to get closer to that ideal. The vision permits the members of the school or district to create a shared image of what the organization could ultimately be.

A few examples of exemplary vision statements from schools and districts in the United States are listed below:

- Bloomfield Hills School District, Bloomfield, Missouri: "Become a nationally recognized Lighthouse District acknowledged for the finest comprehensive curriculum and instruction" (www.bloomfield.org).
- George Mason High School, in Falls Church, Virginia, uses the concept of a "Challenge Statement" in lieu of a vision: "At George Mason we are an exciting and collaborative community of learners who strive toward excellence. We care for each other and take pride in and responsibility for our individual and mutual growth and accomplishments. We celebrate our diversity and seek to foster respect for all in the community through global awareness and application of our individual and cultural differences" (www.fccps.org).
- The vision of Dauphin Island Elementary, in Dauphin Island, Alabama, is "to enable each child to become a productive, responsible citizen prepared for a changing society by nurturing a love of self, respect for others, and a lifelong love of learning. Understanding the naturally inquisitive and creative mind of a child, the dedicated school staff will accomplish this mission in a safe, orderly, and caring atmosphere conducive to learning" (http://dauphin island.mce.schoolinsites.com).
- The vision of Hazelwood School District, in Florissant, Missouri, states, "The Hazelwood School District will be a premier learning community characterized by excellence, equity and high expectations" (http://hsdportal.hazelwood.k12.mo.us/Pages/Default.aspx).

While the vision of the organization allows for dreaming, the mission calls for action. A mission is the purpose of the organization; it is tangible, measurable, and achievable. The mission becomes actualized through goals, the steps that help transform the mission from a statement to a carefully determined series of actions. Finally, an implementation plan is developed in which objectives and strategies to achieve the vision and goals are articulated. This implementation plan should be expressed in such a way that all the stakeholders know and are prepared to work to achieve the beliefs, vision, mission, goals, and plan (exercise 2.1).

The mission should consist of simple action-based words that inspire all members of the organization to take action to ultimately reach the vision of the school or district. A mission is an attainable statement of purpose through which all stakeholders understand how they can contribute to achieving this mission. An effective mission statement should be no longer than a "tweet" or a text message so that it can be easily remembered and restated. A few examples of exemplary mission statements follow:

- The mission of the Hazelwood School District, in Florissant, Missouri, is "to launch learners on a quest for high standards, fairness and distinguished achievement" (http://hsdportal.hazelwood.k12 .mo.us/Pages/Default.aspx).
- The mission statement at Walker's Grove Elementary School in Plainfield, Illinois, is exemplified in the motto "Expect Excellence."
- The Mission of Julian Union Elementary School in Julian, California, is highlighted in a motto that states, "There's a child behind everything we do!" (www.sdcoe.net/districts/julianel).
- Blaine County School District in Bellevue, Idaho, has a mission that states, "To be a world-class, student-focused, community of teaching and learning" (www.blaineschools.org/District/Mission Statement.aspx).

EVERY STUDENT WILL LEARN

Leaders often indicate that their school or district is already ensuring student success. The problem with this concept is how one can assess a vision that is ambiguous and has never been articulated or documented. Even schools or districts that believe they have a strong non-documented vision and mission would find it worthwhile to backward plan. This backward planning will allow for a checkup on whether the stakeholders within the organization are heading in the same direction.

Once the vision is established, an action-oriented mission can be developed that guides goal development and implementation.

An effective vision is designed to ensure that all students are learning. Leaders are advised to "advocate for a specific vision of learning in which every student has equitable, appropriate, and effective learning opportunities and achieves at high levels." By strengthening this standard indicator, leaders can get closer to ensuring an equitable and attainable educational experience for all students. It is not enough to just state our vision, mission, and goals; we need to have everyone within our organizations acting with intentionality to achieve these on a daily basis. According to Stephen Covey, only a small percentage of members of an organization understand or support the organizational vision, mission, or goals. Covey uses the acronym "wigs," which stands for "wildly important goals" (Covey, 2004). What if we embraced this concept within our own educational settings by having our own "wigs" that teachers are passionate about achieving? What would it look like if these "wigs" were constantly at the forefront of everything that we do?

Standard 1 indicator 1I states, "[The leader] advocates for and acts on commitments in the vision, mission, and goals to provide equitable, appropriate, and effective learning opportunities for every student." When developing your vision, mission, and goals, you must ensure that every student is "at the table." This is a figurative description of the necessity to have every student's needs and desires at the forefront of any and all decisions as it relates to such monumental creations such as vision, mission, and goals. Consider alternative ways a leader can demonstrate that the vision, mission, and goals are living and breathing statements. For instance, the vision and mission can be printed in every weekly bulletin to the staff, parent newsletters, meeting agendas, and so on. The goals can also be collaboratively created and then placed on every team-level agenda. The three to four major goals that are created can also be posted on every committee agenda. (A sample team agenda is shown in figure 2.1 at the end of this chapter.) The agenda outline can be shared with teams and committees to use for writing their meeting minutes. This meeting agenda format also allows the leader to quickly address any needs or concerns of the team or committee if they were not able to personally attend the meeting. By utilizing this type of agenda, everyone can commit to and act on the vision, mission, and goals of the organization.

COLLABORATION WITH ALL STAKEHOLDERS

All stakeholders should be actively involved in the creation and implementation of the vision, mission, and goals of the school or district. A leader incorporates diverse perspectives and crafts consensus about vision, mission, and goals that are high yet achievable for every student when provided with suitable, effective learning opportunities. Several processes that can be utilized to help an organization brainstorm, make decisions, and come to consensus on an efficient and effective vision and mission are found in chapter 8. Subsequently, goals must then be established collaboratively to ensure that actions are taken toward meeting each goal. It is very effective to utilize stakeholders when creating or re-creating the vision and mission of the school or district. Individually, each stakeholder may not have the knowledge or tools necessary to develop a mission, vision, or goals, but collectively these dynamic cornerstones can be developed.

Stakeholders provide diverse perspectives in the creation and implementation of the vision and mission. It is important to engage diverse stakeholders, including those with differing perspectives, in ways that build shared understanding and commitment to the vision, mission, and goals. It is nearly impossible to create a vision or mission that addresses diversity unless all stakeholder perspectives are included in the process.

Once a dynamic vision has been established, it is imperative that implementation processes are developed, conducted, and assessed. As stated in the leadership standards, a leader establishes, conducts, and evaluates processes used to engage staff and community in a shared vision, mission, and goals. It is suggested that schools and districts create one process that should be implemented within schools and districts to create ongoing assessments of the vision, mission, and goals. Following are some of the questions that can be asked of the stakeholders in your school or district to assess the success of the vision, mission, and goals. These questions come from Richard DuFour and colleagues' *Learning by Doing: A Handbook for Professional Learning Communities at Work* (2006, p. 142).

1. What evidence do we have that district goals are directly impacting the work of schools and collaborative teams within the school?

_____

_____

_____

2. How do team goals align with district and school goals?

_____

_____

3. Identify one or more team goals that are SMART (specific, measurable, attainable, results oriented, and time bound).

_____

_____

4. How are you monitoring team goals? Provide examples.

_____

_____

_____

5. How are teams provided with relevant and timely feedback regarding their progress? How is this information disseminated? Remember, goals are effective motivators, but only if teams receive feedback.

_____

_____

_____

6. How does your team identify, acknowledge, and celebrate small wins as teams make progress toward their goals?

_____

_____

While doing extensive research on vision, mission, values, and goals, we were surprised to find limited and often nonexistent assessments. It is interesting to note that, even though we value the impact of the development, implementation, and stewarding of the vision, mission, and goals, more ways of assessing the effectiveness of these statements are needed. A rubric has been provided in figure 2.2 at the end of this chapter.

HIGH EXPECTATIONS FOR ALL

Everyone within the organization plays a vital role in the creation, implementation, and stewarding of the school or district vision and mission. A leader communicates and acts from shared vision, mission, and goals so educators and the community understand, support, and act on them consistently. It is important that the leader sustains the passion and excitement for the vision of the organization at the forefront in every way possible. Similar to what was stated earlier about the importance of assessing and evaluating our progress, leaders revise plans, programs, and activities based on systematic evidence and reviews of progress toward the vision, mission, and goals. Once again, it is important to create rubrics to evaluate your plans, programs, and activities, and thus effectively ensure you are still headed toward your vision. Schools and districts typically implement educational programs and do not assess if they are effective or contributing to the vision, mission, and goals.

EXAMINING ASSUMPTIONS AND BELIEFS

Leaders need to have a very good understanding of the assumptions and beliefs that the stakeholders within the organization possess. For instance, parents may assume that all children are succeeding academically within a school environment because their own children are successful. Effective leaders use data to showcase accurate information that can be shown to the stakeholders so they see an accurate picture of the successes and challenges within the school or district. Leadership standard indicator 1J states, "[The leader] uses or develops data systems and other sources of information (e.g., test scores, teacher reports, and student work samples) to identify unique strengths and needs of students, gaps between current outcomes and goals, and areas for improvement." Once the leader identifies these strengths, needs, and gaps, they need to share these with parents and teachers, as well as students, so that everyone has accurate information to reach accurate assumptions.

Beliefs are one of the fundamental components of leadership. For the most part, they are what drive leaders both personally and professionally. Most beliefs are positive and reinforcing, but sometimes they can act as barriers. As an example, we may believe all students can learn. This is an important belief, but it is not enough to believe something; our actions need to ensure that we are achieving our beliefs. In *The Courage to Lead: Choosing the Road Less Traveled*, we shared the concept of "Raising the BAR," which allows leaders to define their *beliefs*, to put their beliefs into *action*, and to continuously *reflect* on the value of the belief (Servais & Sanders, 2006, p. 16). The competent school leader identifies and removes barriers to achieving the vision, mission, and goals. If our beliefs have become a barrier within our organizations, then we need to reflect and determine beliefs that would be more congruent with our vision, mission, and goals.

School and district leaders need to collaboratively create, implement, steward, and assess a vision, a mission, and goals. When all of these pieces align, the organization will be successful: "In these organizations, people are energized by, excited about, and dedicated to such a vision. They have a noble sense of purpose that creates and focuses energy. Their personal values (beliefs) are aligned with the values of the organization. They can describe a clear picture of what they intend to create. Everyone is aligned and going in the same direction" (Blanchard, 2010, p. 10). Move forward with intentionality to improve or build effective visions, missions, and goals, and you will inspire those around you to provide the most outstanding academic environment for every child.

 ## CARING WITH INTENTIONALITY

Take a moment to read the following dispositions and determine a rating for yourself. We challenge you to not only believe strongly in the following dispositions but also take action in what you believe is important. Effective leaders demonstrate congruence between beliefs and actions.

5	4	3	2	1	0
Highly skilled	Proficient	Average	Limited	Little	No skill

Standard 1 Dispositions

Education leaders believe in, value, and are committed to . . .

____ every student learning
____ collaboration with all stakeholders
____ high expectations for all
____ examining assumptions and beliefs

 ASSESSING WITH INTENTIONALITY

Directions

Rate the following items for each standard, with 5 as the highest level of skill ranging to 0 as no skill. Consider your present position and years of leadership experience as you self-assess your performance below. At the end of standard 1, reflect on and identify your strengths and challenges, including a final checkup at the conclusion. Initial preassessment gives you a baseline on your current leadership performance. Once you have completed the exercises provided in *The Courage to Grow*, return to this self-assessment and retake it to measure your leadership growth.

5	4	3	2	1	0
Highly skilled	Proficient	Average	Limited	Little	No skill

Standard 1: Vision, Mission, and Goals

Education leaders ensure the achievement of all students by guiding the development and implementation of a shared vision of learning, strong organizational mission, and high expectations for every student.

Leadership Performance Indicators

Element A: High Expectations for All

A leader . . .

Pre   *Post*

____   ____   uses varied sources of information and analyzes data about current practices and outcomes to shape a vision, mission, and goals with high, measurable expectations for all students and educators. (1A)

____   ____   aligns the vision, mission, and goals to school, district, state, and federal policies (such as content standards and achievement targets). (1B)

____   ____   incorporates diverse perspectives and crafts consensus about vision, mission, and goals that are high and achievable for every student when provided with appropriate, effective learning opportunities. (1C)

____   ____   advocates for a specific vision of learning in which every student has equitable, appropriate, and effective learning opportunities and achieves at high levels. (1D)

Element B: Shared Commitments to Implement the Vision, Mission, and Goals

A leader . . .

____   ____   establishes, conducts, and evaluates processes used to engage staff and community in a shared vision, mission, and goals. (1E)

____   ____   engages diverse stakeholders, including those with conflicting perspectives, in ways that build shared understanding and commitment to vision, mission, and goals. (1F)

____   ____   develops shared commitments and responsibilities that are distributed among staff and the community for making decisions and evaluating actions and outcomes. (1G)

____   ____   communicates and acts from shared vision, mission, and goals so educators and the community understand, support, and act on them consistently. (1H)

_____ _____ advocates for and acts on commitments in the vision, mission, and goals to provide equitable, appropriate, and effective learning opportunities for every student. (1I)

Element C: Continuous Improvement toward the Vision, Mission, and Goals

A leader . . .

_____ _____ uses or develops data systems and other sources of information (e.g., test scores, teacher reports, and student work samples) to identify unique strengths and needs of students, gaps between current outcomes and goals, and areas for improvement. (1J)

_____ _____ makes decisions informed by data, research, and best practices to shape plans, programs, and activities and regularly review their effects. (1K)

_____ _____ uses data to determine effective change strategies and engages staff and community stakeholders in planning and carrying out changes in programs and activities. (1L)

_____ _____ identifies and removes barriers to achieving the vision, mission, and goals. (1M)

_____ _____ incorporates the vision and goals into planning (e.g., strategic plan and school improvement plan), change strategies, and instructional programs. (1N)

_____ _____ obtains and aligns resources (such as learning technologies, staff, time, funding, materials, training, and so on) to achieve the vision, mission, and goals. (1O)

_____ _____ revises plans, programs, and activities based on systematic evidence and reviews progress toward the vision, mission, and goals. (1P)

_____ _____ Standard 1 Total

Standard 1: Leadership Attributes

Personal strengths:

_____
_____
_____

Personal challenges:

_____

_____

_____

 GROWING WITH INTENTIONALITY: BUILDING A SHARED VISION

In order to strengthen your competencies, based on your particular leadership role, review the following exercises. Using the results of your assessment, choose an exercise or two and then write them into the SMART goal format located at the end of this section.

School- and District-Level Administrators

- Collect examples of vision and mission statements from other schools and districts and compare and contrast them. (1A, 1D)
- Invite each district administrator to develop a personal mission, a vision, beliefs, and goals. Share the results with each other. Discuss how each leader's personal leadership mission, vision, beliefs, and goals align with their role within the district. (exercise 2.1, 1E)
- Conduct a book study on vision development using such resources as *The Path* by Laurie Jones. Establish a process to develop or revise the district mission or vision statement. (1A, 1C)
- Identify shared commitments on large poster paper, and then power dot the top commitments. Engage diverse stakeholders in this process. How do these commitments align with the current vision or mission statement? (1E, 1F, 1G)
- Conduct districtwide data reviews across grade levels to ensure that the data is showing continuous improvement (exercise 2.1). Leaders should triangulate data according to the Common Core Standards. (1A, 1J, 1K)

Professors in Educational Administration Programs

- Complete a book study using a vision development book such as *The Path*. (1C)

- Invite each leadership candidate or teacher leader to develop a personal mission, a vision, beliefs, and goals. Share the results with each other. Discuss how each leader's personal leadership mission, vision, beliefs, and goals align with their school role. (exercise 2.2, 1E)
- Identify with future leaders how they can participate in activities within their organizations that relate to vision, mission, and goal development. (1K, 1G)
- Research and share best practices in decision-making, and demonstrate how some decisions can be shared and others may need to be more autocratic. (1K, 1F)
- Have a guest speaker from the district or school level explain how they analyze data as a staff and how they utilize results to improve instruction. Develop an exercise for students to better understand how data can be used to improve instruction in the classroom. (1A, 1J)
- Explain the importance of data walls and data discussions. Utilize exercise 2.1 as an introduction to data discussions and data walls. Additionally, Douglas Reeves has done extensive work on using data walls to drive decision-making. Review his work to give you additional ideas. (1J, 1K, 1L)
- Utilize case studies that illustrate an effective and ineffective organization relevant to vision and mission (e.g., Elaine Wilmore). (1A)

Teacher Leaders or Educational Administration Candidates

- Invite each leadership candidate or teacher leader to develop a personal mission, a vision, beliefs, and goals. Share the results with each other. Discuss how each leader's personal leadership mission, vision, beliefs, and goals align with their school role. (exercise 2.2, 1E)

- Participate in a data-analysis activity. Study and analyze data from your classroom, grade level, department, or school. Prepare a user-friendly means to share the data with your peers. (1J, 1K, 1L)
- Join the school improvement planning committee (or something comparable) to gain a better understanding of how data is gathered, is utilized, and supports the vision and mission of the school or district. (1J, 1L)
- Develop a motto that aligns with the school and district vision and mission. It should be no more than a sentence, easily understandable, and able to be recited by all students and faculty (e.g., "Expect Excellence"; "We Envision, We Seek, We Believe"). (1H, 1N)

INDIVIDUAL LEADERSHIP ACTION PLAN

In each chapter you are asked to create an individual leadership action plan for yourself based on the knowledge and activities that you have learned about. Review your self-assessment results and the "Growing with Intentionality" section and determine some goals that you will establish.

As a result of reading this chapter, I will take the following actions:

I will improve _____ [specific and measurable item] by _____ [what exercises will be used to succeed] by _____ [when]. I will assess my growth by _____ [what type of measurement will be used].

I will improve _____ [specific and measurable item] by _____ [what exercises will be used to succeed] by _____ [when]. I will assess my growth by _____ [what type of measurement will be used].

Figure 2.1. Team Meeting Agenda

Fifth Grade

Expect Excellence

Date _____

Minute Taker_____

S.I.P. Goals:

1. We will improve number sense and applications by ordering and comparing, adding and subtracting, converting equivalents, and demonstrating ratios and proportions for fractions and decimals. We will assess our success monthly using teacher-created data sheets.
2. Grades 3–5: We will improve students' ability to determine the author's purpose in a given passage by the use of discussion in shared reading, guided reading, and intervention groups. We will assess our success monthly using teacher-created data sheets.
3. Grades 4 and 5: We will determine the major and minor details within a given passage by the use of discussion in shared reading, guided reading, and intervention groups. We will assess our success monthly using teacher-created data sheets.

Team Agenda Items:
Team Minutes:
Team Needs or Concerns:
Items for Next Meeting:

VISION, MISSION, BELIEFS, VALUES, AND GOALS RUBRIC

Use the rubric in figure 2.2 to assess your school's/district's vision, mission, beliefs/values, and goals. Provide a score for vision, mission, beliefs/values, and goals. Comments may be provided at the bottom of the rubric. The score reflects the degree of evidence of your five leadership artifacts.

Figure 2.2. Assessment Rubric

Score	Evidence Description	Highly Proficient (5)	Proficient (4)	Average Evidence (3)	Evidence Developing (2)	Lacking or Limited Evidence (1)
	Vision: A statement of aspirations and ideals for the future	The aspirations are vividly stated with great detail	The aspirations are clearly stated	The aspirations are clear	The aspirations are emerging	Lacking all aspirations
	Mission: Statement of the day-to-day purpose of the school; clear, concise, and action-based language	The purpose is well defined; action-based language; clear and concise statement	The purpose is defined; action-based language; clear and concise statement	The purpose is identified; clear statement	The purpose is emerging but not clear and/or concise	The purpose is lacking and unclear
	Belief and Value Statements: Strongly held belief that inspires and impacts behavior; strong values are goal centered in order to produce results and achievement	Eight to ten beliefs or values are very clearly stated as a guide to action	Six to eight beliefs or values are clearly stated as a guide to action	Four to six beliefs or values are identified as a guide to action	Three to four beliefs are emerging as a guide to action	Belief or value statements are provided but lack clarity as a guide to action
	Goals: Actions that illustrate a leader's vision, mission, beliefs, and values; SMART goals (specific, measurable, attainable, results oriented, time bound)	Four to five goals are clearly stated using the five components of SMART goals	Three to four goals are stated using the five components of SMART goals	Two to three goals are stated using a minimum of three components of SMART goals	Two goals are stated using two or more of the components of SMART goals	Goals are limited in clarity and stated in terms lacking SMART components

_____ Total Points

Comments:

Exercise 2.1: Schoolwide Data Activity

This is an activity in which all staff members participate to assist them in understanding how to utilize data in order to establish goals. Break your groups up by department or grade level in order to create more workable groups.

Chunk Code	Does It Relate to Extended Response?
1.4.12 Paraphrase Learning Standard	
Current Grade	Percentage

1. Use a self-adhesive note to first look for areas and standards on the standardized achievement tests where students are performing 70 percent or below.
2. Paraphrase the standard that your students are performing at this percentage point.
3. Write the current grade of the students in the lower left corner of the note.
4. Determine the chunk code (some examples are listed below, but you may create others):

Reading:

V = Vocabulary
PR = Purpose for Reading
CT = Connections to Text
MD = Main Ideas and Details
CH = Characterization
LE = Literary Elements

Math:

M = Measurement
ER = Extended Response
GR = Graphing
GE = Geometry
NS = Number Sense
F = Fractions
D = Data
A = Algebra
MO = Money

5. Once all notes have been created, put them up on poster paper to determine similarities among grade levels; this should lead you to determine your overall school improvement goals for the year ahead.

Exercise 2.2: Beliefs and Vision Action Plan Worksheet

Beliefs

My actions as a leader are based on these beliefs:

_____

_____

Vision

My vision for this organization is as follows:

_____

_____

Mission

My mission to accomplish my beliefs is as follows:

_____

_____

Goals

SMART goals to accomplish my mission (specific, measurable, attainable, results oriented, and time bound) are as follows:

_____

_____

Actions

I will implement my goals in the following way:

_____

_____

CHAPTER 2

LEADERSHIP TOOLS AND RESOURCES FOR GROWTH

Franklin Covey mission builder site:
www.franklincovey.com/msb

SMART goal development:
http://topachievement.com/smart.html
www.achieve-goal-setting-success.com/goal-development.html

Wildly important goals and much more:
www.stephencovey.com

3

A CULTURE FOR LEADING AND LEARNING

Growing What Really Matters

When the team you have doesn't match up to the team of your dreams, then you have only two choices: give up your dream or grow up your team.

—Maxwell, 2001, p. 50

ISLLC STANDARD 2

Education leaders ensure achievement and success of all students by monitoring and continuously improving teaching and learning.

Standard 2 Summary

A strong, positive, professional culture fosters learning by all educators and students. In a strong professional culture, leaders share and distribute responsibilities to provide quality, effectiveness, and coherence across all components of the instructional system (such as curriculum, instructional materials, pedagogy, and student assessment). Leaders are responsible for a professional culture in which learning opportunities are targeted to the vision and goals and differentiated appropriately to meet the needs of every student. Leaders need knowledge, skills, and beliefs that provide equitable differentiation of instruction and curriculum materials to be effective with a range of student characteristics, needs, and achievement.

A strong professional culture includes reflection, timely and specific feedback that improves practice, and support for continuous improvement toward vision and goals for student learning. Educators plan their own professional learning strategically, building their own capacities on the job. Leaders engage in continuous inquiry about effectiveness of curricular and instructional practices and work collaboratively to make appropriate changes that improve results. (Council of Chief State School Officers, 2008, p. 16)

 ## LEARNING WITH INTENTIONALITY

Culture has been defined by many as simply "the way we do things around here" (Barth, 2001, p. 7). However, culture takes into account not only the actions but also the collective values of its members. Gaining a comprehensive understanding of culture requires that members observe well beyond their own limited perspective. A good example of this can be found using the famous Indian legend of the three blind men who came upon an elephant and tried to describe what they found. One approached and touched the elephant's trunk, and identified it as a snake; another touched the elephant's tail, and announced that it was a branch; and a third man found the elephant's ear, and called it a leaf. None could agree on what the elephant looked like since each lacked the perspective of the others. So it is with culture—each person within a school or district will have a different perspective on the culture of the organization; some may be close in their perspectives, and some may have vastly different views. We become so embedded in our views of culture that, much like the three blind men describing the elephant, it would be difficult to imagine anything outside of our current perspectives.

Leaders sometimes struggle to understand culture and how to influence cultural change. Roland Barth has spent much of his career studying culture and summarizes it using a metaphor: "It has been said that a fish would be the last creature on earth to discover water, so totally and continuously immersed in it is he. The same might be said of school people working within their culture" (Barth, 2001, p. 10). Leaders need to understand that change can be difficult when teachers become so immersed in their views of culture. We suggest you visit one of our favorite resources, www.simpletruths.com, and view the video titled "Change Is Good—You Go First." This video provides a valuable reminder of the importance of attitude in our ability to change and serve those around us. Some of the strategies suggested follow: recruit your best people, focus on strengths, believe in each other, simplify, model the behaviors you desire, celebrate successes, measure results, encourage innovation and creativity, stand together and collaborate on the things that matter, and reinforce what matters most and forget the things that don't. These cultural attitudes about change can be found in many resources focusing on healthy organizational cultures.

The competent leader demonstrates knowledge of the functions of the ISLLC standards in order to create and sustain an ideal culture. In this ideal culture, the leader would be able to sustain collaboration, trust, learning, and high expectations. As is noted in the self-assessment at the end of this chapter, the reader needs to have an understanding of each indicator and how these impact their leadership performance. Leaders should have the knowledge to create a comprehensive, rigorous, and coherent curriculum. They should also provide time and resources to build a professional culture of openness and collaboration, engaging teachers in sharing information, analyzing outcomes, and planning improvement. These leaders are committed to ongoing feedback using data, assessments, and evaluation methods that improve practice. Finally, leaders interpret data and communicate progress toward vision, mission, and goals for educators, the school community, and other stakeholders.

LEARNING AS THE FUNDAMENTAL PURPOSE OF SCHOOL

Why is culture so important? The culture of an organization provides the litmus test of what is valued and, consequently, what is the fundamental purpose of the school or district. One school culture may indicate that the fundamental purpose of the school is student learning and would place student achievement at the center of all actions. Another school's purpose may be sustaining the status quo because they don't want to change or risk the comfortable and emotionally safe environment of the adults in the organization. Still another culture may be successful in collectively collaborating with parents, while the next organization's parents are treated as outsiders. The school leader must stand back and view the entire culture, the entire "elephant," in order to make decisions to sustain, minimally change, or radically modify the purpose of the culture.

The competent leader develops a shared understanding and commitment to high expectations for all students. Student achievement has been the primary focus of recent studies by Robert Marzano, Stephen Nettles, and Carolyn Herrington, who have highlighted the impact that leaders play on academic achievement.

> The traditional policy focus regarding student achievement has been on classroom level factors (e.g., scientifically based curricula and teacher quality), and appropriately so, but the national focus is now turning to what the principal can do to improve student achievement. This is a significant redirection, because actions taken to better understand and improve the impact of principals on the achievement of students in their schools have the potential for widespread benefit, as individual improvements in principal practice can impact thousands of students. (Nettles & Herrington, 2007, p. 732)

Leaders play a major role in student success as the federal and state laws continue to emphasize student achievement as the primary indicator of teacher and leader competency.

Knowledge of a healthy culture for learning is all encompassing and may be the most critical area for leader competency. A shift from present culture to the ideal has been suggested by Richard DuFour and colleagues in *Learning by Doing: A Handbook for Professional Learning Communities at Work*. This resource provides an exercise of specific areas that shift organizational culture from a focus on teaching to a focus on learning. This exercise has been included at the end of this chapter and serves as a valuable tool for professional development (exercise 3.1). The culturally competent leader provides support for staff members to examine their own beliefs and practices in relation to the school goals. Members of a healthy culture focus on learning as the primary purpose of the school or district.

DIVERSITY AS AN ASSET

Leaders and staff need to examine their own beliefs and practices as they relate to diversity within the organization. An effective leader provides and monitors differentiated teaching strategies, curricular materials, educational technologies, and other resources appropriate to address diverse student populations. Often, when we have discussions about diversity, we immediately focus on racial and cultural diversity. Leaders need to look at other areas of diversity that exist within their schools. Every child enters school with diverse needs, and it is the leader's responsibility to determine the best ways to address these needs in order to ensure success for all. These issues are addressed more in depth in this chapter as well as in chapter 6.

The need for culturally proficient leaders is even greater in high-poverty schools. Culturally proficient leaders intentionally intersect their own values and beliefs with those of the organization. Leaders in high-poverty schools must overcome deficient thinking often associated with blaming the victim for failure rather than being the influence to challenge and change the culture (Lyman & Villani, 2004). Paulo Freire's work "has illustrated time and again that students and their families are capable of high levels of achievement if they are taught how to learn, provided with the resources to learn, and given a reason to believe that they can control their own destinies" (Lindsey, Robins, & Terrell, 2003, p. 191). Leaders need to advocate for all students and provide adequate resources to assist them in reaching their potential.

The culture of the school can be influenced by focusing on the social and emotional needs of students. In chapter 6 we will go into more detail about diversity and equity; however, one area that needs much more attention in our schools is the social-emotional needs of our students. "This is a fair warning to all administrators: do not dismiss the so-called soft side of students' lives, the social side. It runs their brains, their feelings, and their behaviors—and those three run cognition!" (Jensen, 2009, p. 20). Social-emotional learning plays a large role in student academic achievement.

The influence of social and emotional factors on learning is confirmed by other studies, as well. Based on evidence from 61 educational researchers, 91 meta-analyses, and 179 handbook chapters, Wang, Haertel, and Wallberg (1997) found that social and emotional factors were among the most influential factors on student learning. Particularly high-ranking social and emotional factors included classroom management, parental support, student-teacher social interactions, social-behavioral attributes, motivational-affective attributes, the peer group, school culture, and classroom climate. These experts concluded that directly influencing the psychological components of learning is an effective way of changing how much and how well students learn. (http://casel.org/why-it-matters/benefits-of-sel/sel-academics)

The research and findings of the social and emotional impact on student achievement, particularly regarding poverty, is undisputed. Resources such as Jensen's *Teaching with Poverty in Mind* (2009) are highly encouraged as a faculty book study with discussions about how a school can utilize social-emotional understanding to improve instructional practices. The mandated implementation of social and emotional standards in many states suggests that this may no longer be an option but, rather, a required approach to improve student achievement. Poverty can impact a child's social and emotional development because, "although the effects of poverty are not automatic or fixed, they often set in motion a vicious and stubborn cycle of low expectations. Poor academic performance often leads to diminished expectations, which spread across the board and undermine children's overall self-esteem" (Jensen, 2009, p. 38). One statistic that Jensen highlights is that even though

> most children start school exposed to 5 million words and should know about 13,000 of them . . . that doesn't happen in low-income homes. Weizman and Snow (2001) found that low-income caregivers speak in shorter more grammatically simple sentences. There is less back-and-forth—fewer questions asked and fewer explanations given. As a result, children raised in poverty experience a more limited range of language capabilities. (Jensen, 2009, p. 35)

Poverty is a cyclical problem and can extend over multiple generations. Our job as educators is to learn about best instructional practices to assist students of poverty in order to provide them with every opportunity to achieve academic excellence. Leaders can play a pivotal role in changing the cycle of poverty by finding ways to narrow the achievement gap between the *haves* and the *have nots*. *Best Leadership*

Practices for High-Poverty Schools (Lyman & Villani, 2004) is a resource used in many educational administration preparation programs and is recommended as a book talk for teacher leaders and administrators.

CONTINUOUS PROFESSIONAL GROWTH AND DEVELOPMENT

One way in which leaders can engage faculties in high-quality professional development is to understand and implement the components of adult learning principles. Much has been written about the topic of adult learning theory (Speck, 1996), but many leaders who conduct professional development fail to demonstrate best practices associated with delivering learning opportunities for adults. Learning retention increases with engagement and constructing learning around adult experiences. Leaders who provide professional development need to ensure that the participants are actively engaged in the learning experiences. New knowledge must connect to the experiences participants have had in their own lives. Consider many of the successful teaching strategies in the classroom, and compare these to professional development for adults. The following are examples of positive adult learning practices:

- Learning is maximized with differentiation and awareness of adult learning styles. Similar to the ways in which we teach children, adults also process information through the lens of auditory, kinesthetic/tactile, and visual learning styles. An effective leader needs to incorporate all learning processes into professional development sessions in order to allow all members of the group to understand and ultimately apply the knowledge. Every learning group has diverse learning styles, so professional development needs to be differentiated. Some participants may have a great deal of knowledge about a given subject, but others may be hearing the information for the very first time. Leaders conduct effective staff development by knowing their audience and providing learning experiences that meet all of the participants' needs.
- Learning is directly proportional to the amount of enjoyment adults have in a given learning environment. As we all know, we remember concepts better when we are enjoying ourselves

throughout the learning process. You may recall a time when you remembered various concepts that a teacher was teaching because he or she made the activity more fun and engaging. The same concepts hold true for adult learning. Several engaged learning processes (ELPs) are shared in chapter 8 and throughout the book that will provide enjoyable adult learning experiences.

- Learning does not take place until behavior changes. When we continue to do the same things, we will get the same results. If participants leave a learning session, return to their classrooms or work settings, and do nothing with this knowledge, then it is just as if they had never learned the information. Great leaders will share information through daily or weekly communication that supports the staff development initiatives, thus prompting continuous learning for the faculty or staff.
- Adults are competency based and want to learn skills they can apply pragmatically to their immediate circumstances. How many times have you been in a workshop and thought, "This is not really practical for me in my current position"? Leaders have the responsibility to provide adult learning opportunities that can be put into practice to impact student achievement. Likewise, leaders must acknowledge times when professional development must be differentiated, yet pragmatic, to meet the diverse needs of the adults.

One way of making staff development more effective is to utilize a mini-workshop or menu approach. A mini-workshop may be set up so that everyone rotates through thirty- to forty-minute workshops that relate to a variety of topics. A threefold brochure with learning points could be provided for the participants to take with them to each session and to record notes. A menu can be used where the staff members have options about which learning experiences they will attend. By providing a menu or mini-workshop format, leaders will allow everyone to participate in many activities that relate to their specialty area and best instructional practices.

Successful adult learning will not be accomplished through sedentary or traditional professional development. Rationale for engaged learning can be found in *Brain Rules: 12 Principles for Surviving and Thriving at Work, Home, and School* (Medina, 2008) for leaders to provide creative and interactive activities to activate adult learners. Many ELPs are introduced in chapter 8 that will assist leaders in creating and implementing effective staff development. An effective leader guides and monitors individual professional development plans and progress for continuous improvement of teaching and learning. The growth of strong professional development is vital not only to address the academic needs of the students but also to increase the quality of the learning culture.

LIFELONG LEARNING

A love for learning may be one of the greatest gifts parents and teachers can give to students. A love for learning should be introduced to children at a very young age and has the potential to last a lifetime. Two major influences on a child's love for learning are the parents and the quality of the classroom teacher. Just as teachers are a major influence for children, so does the role of the school leader influence the ability of teachers to learn throughout their careers. Lifelong learning can be intentionally established as a shared cultural value for leaders, students, and staff; this chapter helps leaders to create an environment where lifelong learning is valued.

Teachers need to be aware of their own practices and beliefs regarding learning. One of the main factors influencing student achievement is the classroom teacher. Think about your most influential teacher. Undoubtedly, this person fostered your love of a subject and your desire to learn. In many cases, influential teachers have instilled in their students a desire to become a teacher or leader themselves. Leaders have a responsibility to provide support, time, and resources for staff members to examine their own beliefs, values, and practices for teaching and learning. Once the teachers and staff have examined their own practices and beliefs, they should develop a plan for how they will impact the students' passion for learning.

THREE STEPS TO A HEALTHY LEARNING CULTURE

Culture is not simple, but there are three steps to better understand and improve your organizational culture. First, leaders need to be prudent in their ability to watch, learn, and listen. Leaders must understand what is valued and the history of patterns and rituals that have evolved. Be sure to view the "elephant" from many different angles and gather insights from all stakeholders within the organization.

Second, identify areas of your organizational culture that are toxic or unhealthy to students and teachers. By solving one cultural deficiency, you often create a ripple effect of change that will also impact other related issues. Be patient as you make a single change. Do you remember the game of Pick Up Sticks? Pick up one stick at a time, trying not to disrupt the rest. Little by little, these sticks will separate from one another, and each can be addressed as a single and less complicated issue. This activity is described in more detail in chapter 8.

Third, assess progress toward a healthy cultural development. Consider using the cultural shift inventory (exercise 3.1) to further assess your cultural progress. To assess culture, the leader uses effective data-based technologies and performance management systems to analyze assessment results for accountability and to guide continuous improvement.

 CARING WITH INTENTIONALITY

The competent school leader demonstrates specific dispositions or beliefs according to the ISLLC standards that will assist them in creating the ideal culture. Take a minute to reflect on your own dispositions by assessing yourself in the following areas:

5	4	3	2	1	0
Highly skilled	Proficient	Average	Limited	Little	No skill

Standard 2 Dispositions

Education leaders believe in, value, and are committed to . . .

_____ learning as the fundamental purpose of school
_____ diversity as an asset
_____ continuous professional growth and development

_____ lifelong learning
_____ collaboration with all stakeholders
_____ high expectations for all
_____ student learning

ASSESSING WITH INTENTIONALITY

Directions

Rate the following items for each standard, with 5 as the highest level of skill ranging to 0 as no skill. Consider your present position and years of leadership experience as you self-assess your performance below. At the end of this standard, reflect on and identify your strengths and challenges, including a final checkup at the conclusion. Your initial preassessment gives you a baseline on your current leadership performance. Once you have completed the exercises provided in *The Courage to Grow*, return to this self-assessment and retake it to measure your leadership growth.

5	4	3	2	1	0
Highly skilled	Proficient	Average	Limited	Little	No skill

Standard 2: Teaching and Learning

Education leaders ensure achievement and success of all students by monitoring and continuously improving teaching and learning.

Leadership Performance Indicators

Element A: Strong Professional Culture

A leader . . .

Pre   *Post*

_____   _____   develops shared understanding, capacities, and commitment to high expectations for all students and to closing achievement gaps. (2A)

_____ _____ guides and supports job-embedded, standards-based professional development that improves teaching and learning and meets diverse learning needs of every student. (2B)

_____ _____ models openness to change and collaboration that improves practices and student outcomes. (2C)

_____ _____ develops time and resources to build a professional culture of openness and collaboration, engaging teachers in sharing information, analyzing outcomes, and planning improvement. (2D)

_____ _____ provides support, time, and resources for leaders and staff members to examine their own beliefs, values, and practices in relation to the vision and goals for teaching and learning. (2E)

_____ _____ provides ongoing feedback using data, assessments, and evaluation methods that improve practice. (2F)

_____ _____ guides and monitors individual professional development plans and progress for continuous improvement of teaching and learning. (2G)

Element B: Rigorous Curriculum and Instruction

A leader . . .

_____ _____ develops shared understanding of rigorous curriculum and standards-based instructional programs, working with teams to analyze student work, monitor student progress, and redesign curricular and instructional programs to meet diverse needs. (2H)

_____ _____ provides coherent, effective guidance of rigorous curriculum and instruction, aligning content standards, curriculum, teaching, assessments, professional development, and evaluation methods. (2I)

_____ _____ provides and monitors effects of differentiated teaching strategies, curricular materials, educational technologies, and other resources appropriate to address diverse student populations, including students with disabilities, with cultural and linguistic differences, who are gifted and talented, who come from disadvantaged social-economic backgrounds, or who have other factors affecting learning. (2J)

____ ____ identifies and uses high-quality research and data-based strategies and practices that are appropriate in the local context to increase learning for every student. (2K)

Element C: Assessment and Accountability

A leader . . .

____ ____ develops and appropriately uses aligned, standards-based accountability data to improve the quality of teaching and learning. (2L)

____ ____ uses varied sources and kinds of information and assessments (such as test scores, work samples, and teacher judgment) to evaluate student learning, effective teaching, and program quality. (2M)

____ ____ guides regular analyses and disaggregation of data about all students to improve instructional programs. (2N)

____ ____ uses effective data-based technologies and performance management systems to monitor and analyze assessment results for accountability reporting and to guide continuous improvement. (2O)

____ ____ interprets data and communicates progress toward vision, mission, and goals for educators, the school community, and other stakeholders. (2P)

____ ____ Standard 2 Total

Standard 2: Leadership Attributes

Personal Strengths:

_____

_____

Personal Challenges:

_____

_____

GROWING WITH INTENTIONALITY: BUILDING A CULTURE FOR LEADING AND LEARNING

In order to strengthen your competencies, based on your particular leadership role, review the following exercises. Using the results of your assessment, choose an exercise or two and then write them into the SMART goal format located at the end of this section.

District- and School-Level Administrators

- One sure way that a culture can be studied and improved is through the use of a cultural scavenger hunt or a cultural archeological dig (exercises 3.2 and 3.3). Determine the areas that matter most in your school or district (interventions, differentiation, student engagement, student respect, student achievement, teacher professional development, effective instructional practices, classroom management, parent involvement, etc.). Challenge your staff as teams (grade level or departments) to search out and find evidence that relates to these areas. Provide ample time to seek out and dig up these artifacts and bring them back to share with the rest of the faculty. Observe carefully what is collected and described as valuable. Determine a method of dialogue that can occur based on this collection of cultural artifacts. Keep this collection of artifacts or write up a list of the items collected and the rationale of their importance. As an example, one principal saved these items and placed them in a school portfolio that was shared with parents, students, district-level administrators, board members, and teachers. (2B)
- Repeat this scavenger hunt or archeological dig activity each year, and note the type of artifacts collected and rationale of their importance. Has your culture grown or changed? (2B, 2L)
- Conduct a personality-type preference inventory. A great deal of work has been done on the use of personality type and its impact on culture, collaboration, and community development. The use of personality-type preferences allows leaders to view their staffs through a different lens in order to gain a more comprehensive view of the culture. Most leaders do not doubt

they have a faculty with diverse personalities. However, this is nothing more than another blind spot if individuals or leaders do not understand what these patterns and personalities mean for the culture. You can obtain the personality-type inventory from many websites (e.g., www.keirsey.com) and review print resources such as *Differentiated School Leadership* (Kise & Russell, 2007). (2E, 2G)

- Identify your school and district improvement goals, and assess how your learning culture supports achieving these goals. (2D, 2H)

Educational Leadership Professors

- Provide opportunities for the leadership candidates in your classes to share insights into their individual cultures. By understanding the diverse cultures that currently exist in school, professors can embed appropriate instructional strategies to assist students in understanding current cultural realities. (2D, 2F)
- Add the book *Best Leadership Practices for High-Poverty Schools* or *Teaching with Poverty in Mind* to your required text list to enrich student understanding of diversity. (2A)
- Assign students the scavenger hunt and archeological search activities (exercises 3.2 and 3.3) as a means to define their current cultures. Share the results with the class. This activity allows all members of your class to understand different cultures. It also provides your students with an insight into their current culture that they may not have previously understood. (2B)
- Review and analyze current research on educational culture to update yourself on the most recent cultural issues. As a means to enhance your cultural understanding, meet regularly with school and district partnership leaders to discuss the current realities of their school's cultural setting. (2K)

Leadership Candidates and Teacher Leaders

- Conduct a school-based scavenger hunt and archeological search (exercises 3.2 and 3.3) to gain an increased awareness of not only the school's culture but also the culture of your team or department. (2B)

- Initiate a book talk on *Best Leadership Practices for High-Poverty Schools* or *Teaching with Poverty in Mind* for your grade level or department as a means to better understand these cultural issues. (2A)
- Dialogue with individual members of the school community to gain a greater insight into the views of all staff members. We often segregate ourselves into small team-based cultures and assume that the rest of the school personnel believe in and see the same cultural issues, whereas in reality views can be very different. Note the similarities and differences defined in your dialogue. (2C)
- Complete the bridge activity as a means to understand present culture and how we need to bridge between current and future cultural issues (exercise 3.4). (2B, 2G)

INDIVIDUAL LEADERSHIP ACTION PLAN

In each chapter you are asked to create an individual leadership action plan for yourself based on the knowledge and activities you have learned about. Review your self-assessment results and the "Growing with Intentionality" section and determine some goals that you will establish.

As a result of reading this chapter, I will take the following actions:

I will improve _____ [specific and measurable item] by _____ [what exercises will be used to succeed] by _____ [when]. I will assess my growth by _____ [what type of measurement will be used].

I will improve _____ [specific and measurable item] by _____ [what exercises will be used to succeed] by _____ [when]. I will assess my growth by _____ [what type of measurement will be used].

EXERCISE 3.1: CULTURAL SHIFTS IN A PROFESSIONAL LEARNING COMMUNITY

Directions

Please complete the following survey independently. Your candid opinion on this survey will allow the school improvement planning/ professional learning community (SIP/PLC) committees to make decisions for future staff development based on your input. Circle the number that aligns closest to where you feel we are as a school or district with a 1 being closer to the statement on the left and a 5 being closer to the statement on the right. This activity is derived from *Learning by Doing: A Handbook for Professional Learning Communities at Work* (DuFour, DuFour, Eaker, & Many, 2006).

A Shift in Fundamental Purpose

Focus on teaching	1	2	3	4	5	Focus on learning
Coverage of content	1	2	3	4	5	Demonstration of proficiency
Providing individual teachers with curriculum documents such as state standards and curriculum guides	1	2	3	4	5	Engaging collaborative teams in building shared knowledge regarding essential curriculum

A Shift in Use of Assessments

Infrequent summative assessments	1	2	3	4	5	Frequent common formative assessments
Assessments to determine which students failed to learn by the deadline	1	2	3	4	5	Assessments to identify students who need additional time and support

Each teacher determines the criteria to be used in assessing student work	1	2	3	4	5	Collaborative teams clarify the criteria and ensure consistency among team members when assessing student work
Focusing on average scores	1	2	3	4	5	Monitoring each student's proficiency in every essential skill

A Shift in the Response When Students Don't Learn

Individual teachers determining the appropriate response	1	2	3	4	5	A systematic response that ensures support for every student
One opportunity to demonstrate learning	1	2	3	4	5	Multiple opportunities to demonstrate learning

A Shift in the Work of Teachers

Each teacher determining pacing of the curriculum	1	2	3	4	5	Collaborative teams agreeing on common pacing
Individual teachers attempting to discover ways to improve results	1	2	3	4	5	Collaborative teams helping each other improve
Assumptions that "these are my kids; those are your kids"	1	2	3	4	5	These are "our kids"

A Shift in Focus

	1	2	3	4	5	
External focus on issues outside of the school	1	2	3	4	5	Internal focus on steps the staff can take to improve the school
Teachers gathering data from individually constructed tests in order to assign grades	1	2	3	4	5	Collaborative teams using common assessments to (1) inform their individual and collective practice, and (2) respond to students who need additional time and support

A Shift in School Culture

	1	2	3	4	5	
Language of complaint	1	2	3	4	5	Language of commitment
Long-term strategic planning	1	2	3	4	5	Planning for short-term wins

A Shift in Professional Development

	1	2	3	4	5	
Expectations that learning occurs infrequently (on the few days devoted to professional development)	1	2	3	4	5	Expectation that learning is ongoing and occurs as part of routine work practice
Presentations to entire faculty	1	2	3	4	5	Team-based action research
Short-term exposure to multiple concepts and practices	1	2	3	4	5	Sustained commitment to limited, focused initiatives

EXERCISE 3.2: SCAVENGER HUNT

I. Each grade-level team or department needs to search for five cultural or instructional artifacts. Teams can choose five of the ten artifacts.
- Team artifact
- Curricular artifact
- Intervention artifact
- Assessment artifact
- Student product artifact
- Student engagement artifact
- School/community partnership artifact
- Classroom management artifact
- Communication artifact
- Free choice artifact

II. Once teams or departments have identified and collected their artifacts, they should write a reflective statement on how this artifact illustrates the school's success.

III. When we return as a staff, each group needs to share their artifact collection and explain each item.

IV. A school portfolio is then created from all of these artifacts.

EXERCISE 3.3: CONDUCTING AN ARCHEOLOGICAL SEARCH FOR CULTURE

Directions

You have been hired to conduct an archeological search of evidence of your school culture and the culture of one of the teams within your organization. A list of possible artifacts or evidence is shown in table 3.1. Describe the evidence you find as you dig beyond the surface of your culture.

Table 3.1. Archeological Search for Culture—Results

Cultural Evidence and Artifacts	Team Findings	Organization/School Community Findings
Physical environment (space priorities, colors, learning structures, decorations, displays, etc.)		
Language/Communication (name, mission statement, vision, newsletters, greetings, banners, meeting management, diversity, networking, stories, etc.)		
Customs/Traditions (beginnings, historical events, past achievements, music, programs, professional development, etc.)		
Favorite symbols (mascot, logos, artwork, trophies, etc.)		
Celebrations (special events, accomplishments, recognition programs, etc.)		

Cultural Assessment

1. What were the norms discovered through evidence and artifacts of team culture? Organizational culture?
2. What did you discover about what is valued most among the team? The organization?
3. What evidence did you uncover that was a surprise?
4. What evidence reinforced the existing norms of the team or organizational culture?
5. What is a possible new symbol, event, or celebration that you may want to consider to enhance the future organizational culture?

EXERCISE 3.4: BRIDGING CULTURAL CHANGE

Sample Directions

Teams or departments should identify their present cultural best practices in the left column of the bridge. Next, they need to discuss and write their dream best practices in the area of cultural enhancements inside the right column. Once the participants have identified their present and future best cultural practices, they need to brainstorm potential strategies to make their ideal culture a reality and list them in the middle column.

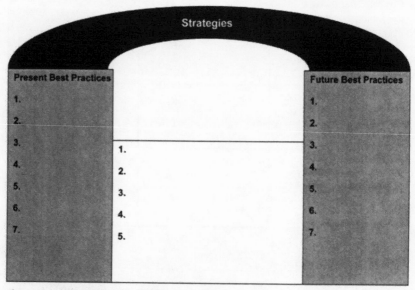

Figure 3.1. Strategies for Bridging Cultural Change

LEADERSHIP TOOLS AND RESOURCES FOR GROWTH

Collaborative for Academic, Social, and Emotional Learning:
http://casel.org/why-it-matters/benefits-of-sel/sel-academics

Simple Truths website full of inspirational videos and books:
www.simpletruths.com

One website devoted to personality assessments:
www.keirsey.com

Website devoted to improving cultural practices:
www.schoolculture.net

Solution Tree:
www.solution-tree.com

4

MANAGING AND LEADING

The Balancing Act to Optimize Learning

Collaborative leaders are interpersonal and interinstitutional relationship mangers who build bridges with others to do work better, faster, more easily, more enduringly, more efficiently, with bigger impact, with broader ownership, and with higher meaning.

—Rubin, 2002, p. 14

ISLLC STANDARD 3

Education leaders ensure the success of all students by managing organizational systems and resources for a safe, high-performing learning environment.

Standard 3 Summary

Traditionally, school leaders focused on the management of a school or school district. A well-run school where buses run on time, the facility is clean, and the halls are orderly and quiet used to be the mark of an effective school leader. With the shift to leadership for learning, maintaining an orderly environment is necessary but not sufficient to meet the expectations and accountability requirements facing educators today.

Education leaders need a systems approach in complex organizations of schools and districts. In order to ensure the success of all students and provide a high-performing learning environment, education leaders manage daily operations and environments through efficiently and effectively aligning resources with vision and goals. Valuable resources include financial, human, time, materials, technology, physical plant, and other system components.

Leaders identify and allocate resources equitably to address the unique academic, physical, and mental health needs of all students. Leaders address any conditions that might impede student and staff learning, and they implement laws and policies that protect the safety of students and staff members. They promote and maintain a trustworthy, professional work environment by fulfilling their legal responsibilities, enacting appropriate policies, supporting due process, and protecting civil and human rights of all. (Council of Chief State School Officers, 2008, p. 19)

 ## LEARNING WITH INTENTIONALITY

Leadership has been described as doing the right things, and management has been described as doing things right. These two vital roles can be compared to the use of our right and left hand. Each is needed, although for certain tasks many of us choose to use our dominant hand. It would not be logical to suggest that we can only use our dominant hand, just as it is not logical to choose between the importance of leadership and management. On any given day, an effective administrator needs to balance the dichotomous roles as a leader and manager in addressing student success in organizational systems and disbursing resources for a high-performing learning environment.

The effective leader skillfully combines many factors to manage a safe and successful learning environment. Safety includes almost every aspect of a school to support the learning of every student. The leader maintains the physical plant for safety, develops and facilitates communication and data systems that ensure the timely flow of information, and maintains equipment and effective technologies.

The successful leader could be compared to the successful band conductor. Like the band conductor, a leader must facilitate collaboration from each musician to masterfully blend all the instruments to achieve a harmonious combination of notes to ultimately create a masterpiece. Among the instrumental blend, the leader seeks in standard 3 to design processes to effectively manage a safe and supportive learning environment whereby resources are equitably distributed to address the needs and culture of a school community. The school improvement plan, the blueprint for school goals and areas for improvement, should be one of the first areas considered in resource distribution. To accomplish the indicators of standard 3, a leader must understand and implement processes to align resources with the culture and goals of a school community. One of the great responsibilities of a leader is to recruit and retain highly qualified staff. A culture of shared goals, beliefs, and values must serve as the focus for the resources of the organization. Other areas of focus may be found in the district strategic plan, schoolwide initiatives, and state policies. Processes are needed to include teachers, parents, and students as participants in the development and achievement of norms and guidelines. A transparent process for stakeholders to share leadership opportunities and resources may ultimately determine the degree of commitment to carry out the goals of the organization. In summary, standard 3 begins with the issues of safety, including alignment and management of human and fiscal resources, and culminates with the continued stewardship of the organization's mission and vision.

Organizational management is about effective use of both financial and human resources. One of the most essential management styles for leaders is relational management. Two leadership styles are common in managing relationships and, ultimately, human resources. James MacGregor Burns (1978) coined the terms "transformational" and "transactional" as two distinct but complementary leadership styles. The transformational leader demonstrates a high value for building relationships with shared commitments and goals that are mutually satisfying to the members and leaders. Transactional leadership, on the other hand, is an exchange of something of value the leader possesses or controls with something the followers want in return for their services. Ideally, a leader must be both transformational and transactional to be successful. The effective leader determines which style is best suited in the myriad of leadership situations that are encountered. Transactional situations call for a leader to manage and negotiate the completion of tasks among faculty and staff members, students, and the community. The transformational leader unites and inspires stakeholders to develop a caring, efficient, and effective learning community, the essential components of leadership standard 3.

Chapter 4 addresses ways for leaders to balance the management of relationships, communication, time, space, and resources. Often these resources take the form of the school budget, classroom space allocations, communication, calendars, meetings, and professional development for teachers. This chapter identifies ways to demonstrate the roles associated with leadership and management to maximize a safe, caring, and effective environment for learning.

A SAFE AND SUPPORTIVE LEARNING ENVIRONMENT

A safe and supportive learning environment is at the center of any successful school. Yet leaders may find themselves managing a learning community where caring and compassion are viewed as not essential to the daily operations. The National School Climate Council (2007) recommends the essential components of a safe and supportive climate:

> A sustainable, positive school climate fosters youth development and learning necessary for a productive, contributing and satisfying life in a democratic society. This climate includes norms, values and expectations that support people feeling socially, emotionally and physically safe. People are engaged and respected. Students, families and educators work together to develop, live and contribute to a shared school vision. Educators' model and nurture attitudes that emphasize the benefits and satisfaction gained from learning. Each person contributes to the operations of the school and the care of the physical environment. (www .schoolclimate.org/guidelines)

The social and emotional standards are being implemented to sustain a safe and supportive learning environment. Social and emotional learning (SEL) is threaded throughout the standards. It is the process through which children develop awareness and management of their emotions, set and achieve important personal and academic goals, use social awareness and interpersonal skills to establish and maintain positive relationships, and demonstrate decision-making and responsible behaviors to achieve school and life success. The Illinois Children's Mental Health Act of 2003 required the Illinois State Board of Education (ISBE) to develop SEL standards as essential K–12 curriculum and part of the Illinois Learning Standards. The standards have been developed in accordance with Section 15(a) of Public Act 93-0495. This act calls upon the Illinois State Board of Education (n.d.) to "develop and implement a plan to incorporate social and emotional development standards as part of the Illinois Learning Standards."

It is important to remind educators of the value of caring and compassion as it relates to relationship building in high-performing schools. The well-known works of Nel Noddings (2005) suggest the need for students to feel that at least one adult cares for them before students can reciprocate in caring about learning and each other. An atmosphere of caring is built on the premise that schools are a center of caring and provide stability and continuity for learning in small groups from adults as student advocates (Noddings, 2005). School leaders must, therefore, find systematic ways for teachers, students, and parents to demonstrate caring and respect for each other.

Consider that the need for quality schools may rest on this ideal: the quality of relationships determines the quality of schools. Where can high-quality and caring relationships be found in your school? The Illinois Children's Mental Health Partnership (ICMHP) is among many resources available to school leaders to improve the scope, quality, and access of mental health programs. The partnership (n.d.) believes that a comprehensive, coordinated approach to healthy social and emotional development, prevention, early intervention, and treatment helps children and their families live healthier, happier lives with a better chance for a brighter future. A purposeful leader that manages relationships and has a sense of connectedness for individuals within the community becomes an integral part of the compassion and caring found in schools (Noddings, 2005).

The transformational leader naturally models collaboration and relationship management. Collaboration is an intentional and systematic approach to align people's actions to meet the organizational goals: "Collaborative leaders are interpersonal and interinstitutional relationship mangers" who build bridges with others to do work "better, faster, more easily, more enduringly, more efficiently, with bigger impact, with broader ownership, and with higher meaning" (Rubin, 2002, p. 14). Think about the leaders you have seen who intentionally build bridges of positive social interactions. Consider the strategies you would use to be a relationship manager. The transformational leader, who values and strives to continuously develop relationships within the school, will provide a caring environment for teachers, parents, and students.

MANAGEMENT TO SERVICE STAFF
AND STUDENT LEARNING

An effective leader must know and be able to meet the needs of faculty members, staff members, and students within the learning community. It is vital, therefore, that the school leader is able to effectively communicate with all members of a community. The effective leader's communication will intentionally underscore the vision, mission, and purpose of the organization. Equally vital is that each member of the community must understand the role that is expected of him or her to achieve the mission and ensure the success of all students. Many types of communication are needed to address the complex personnel issues within a successful learning environment. Not only are the varied types of communication important but also the consistency of the leader's words and actions: "Leaders must realize that the most important element in communicating is congruency between their actions and their words. It is not essential that leaders are eloquent or clever; it is imperative, however, that they demonstrate consistency between what they say and what they do" (DuFour, DuFour, Eaker, & Many, 2006, p. 28).

Management of communication can be found in many schools today, particularly within professional learning communities (PLCs). The primary purposes of communication in a professional learning community are learning, collaborative teams, and the essential dynamics of a learning community. A PLC leader provides clear communication regarding the four pillars of a community: vision, mission, values, and goals (DuFour, DuFour, Eaker, & Many, 2006). Collaborative teaching teams share in communicating student-centered values and monitor priorities for learning for all its members. In order for teaching teams to be successful, communication must be modeled, practiced, and supported. Systematic approaches to improve team communication, problem solving, and decision-making are addressed in this chapter. High-performing learning environments utilize clear, continuous, and reciprocal communication by the leader and all stakeholders.

OPERATING EFFICIENTLY AND EFFECTIVELY

Leadership is the meticulous balance and alignment of resources to maximize efficiency and effectiveness in the daily operation of a school community. Some of these areas include the management of the physical plant, the master schedule, parents as partners, and professional development for faculty. The school facility must be under the careful watch of the school leader and those delegated to be responsible for its safe, daily operation. Daily operations must support the functions of a high-performing learning environment, planning and practicing for safety drills and possible disruptions to the operation of the school. The development, implementation, and management of the school schedule are among the many areas that contribute to the effectiveness of the daily instructional operations. School discipline is another area of management that must be well defined and structured to address a wide range of student behavior and academic needs. The leader must provide training and preparation for staff to address the dynamic social and academic needs of students. Parents are valued as partners and play an active role in the daily effective and efficient functions of the school. When learning does not occur, instruction is modified and teachers are provided with professional development as needed. Response to Intervention (RtI) is the most recent example of teachers learning ways to offer academic or behavioral interventions to ensure student success.

Effective instruction is among a school's greatest resource as a means to impact student achievement (Danielson, 2007). One of the top professional resources for the instructional leader to consider to improve teacher supervision has come from the work of Charlotte Danielson. Danielson identifies that an effective system of teacher evaluation accomplishes two things: it ensures quality teaching, and it promotes professional learning. Effective leaders recognize that the quality of teaching is the single most important determinant of student learning. It must be among the highest priorities for a school district to establish a system of teacher evaluation in order to ensure high-quality teaching (Danielson, 2007). Leaders are responsible for managing systems of effective hiring, supervision, and evaluation of teachers in order to maximize the quality of instruction found in schools. The development and management of processes to supervise and evaluate teachers remain a challenge for many school leaders. Not only is teacher supervision complex, but it is also very time consuming for the school leader, who already faces many demands.

Among all of the resources important to the management of a school environment, one of the most valued is time. The leader who utilizes time efficiently gains support and confidence from teachers and parents. Tasks that must be completed are carefully calculated to be sure they support students, learning, and school goals. Tasks are monitored and, when necessary, eliminated by the leader, knowing that time is a limited resource. The effective leader looks at time much like the management of the game clock in a football game, where every minute counts. Time management is demonstrated in a school community by carefully planned meetings, professional development, curriculum development, instruction, assessment of learning, and data-based interventions to improve learning.

Efficient management practices need to be understood and implemented in order to conduct effective meetings. Hundreds of meetings are held in schools throughout the year. For the instructional leader, meetings are his or her classroom. The leader knows that meetings, much like classrooms, need to be well planned and managed. These are in the form of faculty meetings, grade-level or team meetings, district office meetings, department meetings, professional development days, and any occasion when teachers are called together. Unfortunately, teachers frequently describe school meetings as poorly planned and conducted. Even more alarming are the descriptions given by principals of district office meetings implemented by administrators who have little or no competence in conducting effective meetings. As a result, time is wasted and meeting participants become less confident in the ability to achieve the organizational goals and values. Meetings are frequently described as having no clear purpose, poor planning, off-task behaviors, poor use of time, inconclusive results, and nonengagement by the participants. Meetings become viewed as unproductive and a waste of time, a situation that is painfully endured.

Effective meeting management is one of the primary ways for an organization to maximize time as a resource. The following six steps are a combination of many resources on this topic. These should be considered practical and universal strategies to plan and implement effective meetings:

1. Develop and utilize an agenda with clearly defined goals. Rule of thumb: no agenda—no meeting.
2. Identify, maintain, and revise guiding principles or norms as needed. These are three to five "rules" that serve as norms to establish and guide a team's work and influence the behavior of the members. Sample guiding principles: listen to understand, not to contradict; ask questions to check for understanding; challenge ideas, not people; everyone is expected to participate and contribute; agree to disagree—agreeably; and enjoy each other.
3. Identify roles and responsibilities of the members. Tap into the strengths and talents of each person. Common primary roles: facilitator, recorder, time keeper, and task manager.
4. Define the purpose of each agenda item: information, discussion, or decision. Place a time restriction on each. Items that are information only should be short in duration. Topics that require discussion may be placed on the agenda more than once but eventually must be brought to a point of decision-making.
5. Before moving to the next agenda topic, an effective facilitator summarizes the item that has been discussed and expected outcomes. This provides clarity for both persons in attendance and the recorder. The time and effort to summarize each point is well worth it to most groups who otherwise may still be ambiguous about the outcome of each agenda topic.
6. Define problems clearly and allow the team to provide suggestions. Determine the best outcome by consensus when possible. Table items only when absolutely necessary, as it delays action and must return to the next agenda.
7. Utilize a "parking lot" for topics that are brought up during the meeting that are not a part of the agenda. This recognizes

the importance of a good idea but does not derail the planned agenda. Items placed in the "parking lot" should be added to one of the next agendas.

8. Provide minutes and written outcomes of the meeting as evidence of what was discussed and accomplished.

Leaders may wish to consider the Golden Rule as the single most important principle to consider when conducting meetings: run your meetings as you would have others run the meetings you attend. Many resources are available to leaders to conduct effective meetings. Two favorite resources are Glenn Parker and Robert Hoffman's (2006) *Meeting Excellence: 33 Tools to Lead Meetings that Get Results* and the website http://effectivemeetings.com. Running an effective meeting demonstrates good utilization of time, a valuable resource for all.

COLLABORATION WITH ALL STAKEHOLDERS

Collaborative leaders communicate well with organizational members in the development, implementation, and management of school goals and decisions. The complex problems schools face today cannot be addressed by single leadership or by a committed few. Rather, the effective leader invites all teachers, parents, and students to have an active voice and participate in carrying out shared goals, operations, decision-making, and (ultimately) the celebration of successes. The teaming structure is among the most important organizational management tasks to create a schoolwide system of collaboration and shared decision-making.

Teams are a microcosm of the organization. Effective teaming practices have been addressed in detail in *The Courage to Lead: Choosing the Road Less Traveled.*

Teams are created to achieve specific organizational tasks and goals. Teaming provides opportunities for organizations to reach heights that could not be accomplished by individuals working alone. Teams may be identified as committees, task forces, departments, grade-level teams, community partnerships, boards, councils, home school partnerships, and district leadership teams. Regardless of what teams are called within an organization, they are each created for a defined purpose. In addition to teams having a technical purpose, they also contribute to the socialization and the satisfaction people experience when they work together toward a common goal. (Servais & Sanders, 2006, p. 68)

The effective leader incorporates and manages teaming into the system in order to provide structures for stakeholders to collaborate and achieve the organizational goals.

EQUITABLE DISTRIBUTION OF RESOURCES

A resource can be defined as any physical or virtual entity of limited availability that needs to be consumed to obtain a benefit from it. In most cases, the physical environment, personnel, and time are factors that must be considered within the allocation of a school's resources. Often a gap exists between the goals and values of a school community and standard 3's component of equitable distribution of resources. This gap occurs for a variety of reasons. One of the main gaps relates to issues of equity and is often overshadowed by policies to provide equal resources to schools regardless of diverse needs. Failure to allocate resources aligned with the genuine needs of a school result in the perpetuation of an achievement gap within a school and district. An effective leader advocates for the resources necessary to ensure success for each student and seeks and secures additional resources needed to accomplish the vision and goals. Chapter 6 explores issues of equity and equitable distribution of resources.

Standard 3 reminds leaders of the importance of both leadership and management in order to ensure the success of all students by managing organizational systems and resources for a safe, high-performing learning environment. While there is no algorithm for leadership, the standards provide a good template for which school leaders can mold their own behavior and performance.

CARING WITH INTENTIONALITY

Take a moment to read the following dispositions and determine a rating for yourself. We challenge you to not only believe strongly in the following dispositions but also take action in what you believe is important.

Dispositions Exemplified in Standard 3

5	4	3	2	1	0
Highly skilled	Proficient	Average	Limited	Little	No skill

The education leader believes in, values, and is committed to . . .

_____ a safe and supportive learning environment
_____ collaboration with all stakeholders
_____ equitable distribution of resources
_____ operating efficiently and effectively
_____ management in service of staff and student learning

 ASSESSING WITH INTENTIONALITY

Directions

Rate the following items for each standard, with 5 as the highest level of skill ranging to 0 as no skill. Consider your present position and years of leadership experience as you self-assess your performance below. At the end of each standard, reflect on and identify your strengths and challenges, including a final checkup at the conclusion. Your initial preassessment gives you a baseline on your current leadership performance. Once you have completed the exercises provided in *The Courage to Grow*, return to this self-assessment and retake it to measure your leadership growth.

5	4	3	2	1	0
Highly skilled	Proficient	Average	Limited	Little	No skill

Standard 3: Managing Organizational Systems and Safety

Education leaders ensure the success of all students by managing organizational systems and resources for a safe, high-performing learning environment.

Leadership Performance Indicators

Element A: Effective Operational Systems

A leader . . .

Pre   *Post*

____   ____   uses effective tools such as problem-solving skills and knowledge of strategic, long-range, and operational planning to continuously improve the operational system. (3A)

____   ____   maintains the physical plant for safety, ADA requirements, and other access issues to support learning of every student. (3B)

____   ____   develops and facilitates communication and data systems that ensure the timely flow of information. (3C)

____   ____   oversees acquisition and maintenance of equipment and effective technologies, particularly to support teaching and learning. (3D)

____   ____   distributes and oversees responsibilities for leadership of operational systems. (3E)

____   ____   evaluates and revises processes to continuously improve the operational system. (3F)

Element B: Aligned Fiscal and Human Resources

A leader . . .

____   ____   operates within budget and fiscal guidelines and directs them effectively toward teaching and learning. (3G)

____   ____   allocates funds based on student needs within the framework of federal and state rules. (3H)

____   ____   aligns resources (such as time, people, space, and money) to achieve the vision and goals. (3I)

____   ____   implements practices to recruit and retain highly qualified personnel. (3J)

____ ____ assigns personnel to address diverse student needs, legal requirements, and equity goals. (3K)

____ ____ conducts personnel evaluation processes that enhance professional practice, in keeping with district and state policies. (3L)

____ ____ seeks and secures additional resources needed to accomplish the vision and goals. (3M)

Element C: Protecting the Welfare and Safety of Students and Staff

A leader . . .

____ ____ advocates for and creates collaborative systems and distributed leadership responsibilities that support student and staff learning and well-being. (3N)

____ ____ involves parents, teachers, and students in developing, implementing, and monitoring guidelines and norms for accountable behavior. (3O)

____ ____ develops and monitors a comprehensive safety and security plan. (3P)

____ ____ Standard 3 Total

Standard 3 Leadership Attributes

Personal Strengths:

_____
_____
_____

Personal Challenges:

_____
_____
_____

GROWING WITH INTENTIONALITY:
MANAGING AND LEADING

In order to strengthen your competencies, based on your particular leadership role, review the following exercises. Using the results of your assessment, choose an exercise or two and then write them into the SMART goal format located at the end of this section.

District- and School-Level Administrators

- Conduct a physical plant assessment. You should be able to obtain a copy of an assessment from the business and operations department in your district or do an online search. (3B, 3F)
- Develop a one-hundred-day plan for a school goal or initiative. (3F, 3N)
- Complete exercise 4.1 as an activity that assists in analyzing how resources are distributed within your school or district. (3I, 3A)
- Review or revise your school or district safety and crisis plans. In order to create a comprehensive plan, gather input from police and fire agencies to ensure that you have the most up-to-date procedures. (3P, 3O)
- Review recruiting procedures as well as retention procedures such as mentoring programs. (3K, 3J)
- Review and analyze teacher evaluation plans and procedures, and highlight strengths or weaknesses of current practices. Additionally, input should be gathered by teachers to determine their views on the current evaluation procedures, ensuring that you are meeting their learning needs. (3L, 3N)
- Conduct a resource four-square activity in these areas: time, personnel, space, and funding (exercise 4.2). From the district level, review a new initiative that you currently have in place; then answer the following questions: (1) How have you allotted time for this initiative? (2) How have you allotted personnel to

implement this initiative? (3) How have you allotted space for this initiative? (4) How have you financially supported this initiative? (3G, 3H)

- Review a walk-through model that may work for you and your organization. Caroline Downey (2004) has written extensively on the three-minute walk-through as well as additional models associated with the effectiveness of walk-throughs. Also research the Instructional Practices Inventory created by Jerry Valentine (2005), and determine its potential effectiveness in your school or district. Exercise 4.3 highlights an effective walk-through format that you can implement. (3N, 3L)

Professors in Educational Administration Programs

- Assign a project where a candidate could shadow and practice skills for analyzing effective teachers (e.g., observe a fellow teacher, or shadow an administrator during a formal evaluation). Have the candidate use the same evaluation tool that the district uses, and compare and contrast these evaluations with the administrator. (3K, 3L)
- Plan an activity where the candidates need to conduct a physical plant assessment of their own school facility, and then bring the results back to the class and discuss the findings. This should be done in a management and operations class and or a facilities course. (3B, 3F)
- Conduct a resource four-square activity in these areas: time, personnel, space, and funding (exercise 4.2). From the district level, review a new initiative that you currently have in place; then answer the following questions: (1) How have you allotted time for this initiative? (2) How have you allotted personnel to implement this initiative? (3) How have you allotted space for this initiative? (4) How have you financially supported this initiative? (3G, 3H)

Leadership Candidates and Teacher Leaders

- Complete exercise 4.1 to assist in analyzing how resources are distributed within your school or district. (3I, 3A)
- Conduct a resource four-square activity in these areas: time, personnel, space, and funding (exercise 4.2). From the district level,

review a new initiative that you currently have in place; then answer the following questions: (1) How have you allotted time for this initiative? (2) How have you allotted personnel to implement this initiative? (3) How have you allotted space for this initiative? (4) How have you financially supported this initiative? (3G, 3H)

- Conduct an evaluation of your colleagues. Ask your administrator if you can shadow them throughout an evaluation cycle with a colleague. Generally, colleagues have no problem with having a future administrator sit in on a preobservation conference, observation, and postobservation conference. To get the most out of the experience, you should actually use the district's teacher observation form and fill one out while you are in for the actual observation. Have your administrator critique your write-up, and, if you feel comfortable, actually share some of your observations during the postevaluation conference. (3L, 3J)
- Review and analyze the school or district budget. How does the budget support the school or district improvement goals and other initiatives? Be aware of how the budget reflects the equity and diversity needs in the district. (3G, 3H, 3I)
- Make an appointment with the district business manager or the assistant superintendent of business and operations to ask them questions about budget allocations and utilization of resources. (3G, 3H, 3I)
- Review a walk-through model that may work for you and your organization. Caroline Downey has written extensively on the three-minute walk-through as well as additional models associated with the effectiveness of walk-throughs. Also research the Instructional Practices Inventory created by Jerry Valentine, and determine its potential effectiveness in your school or district. Exercise 4.3 highlights an effective walk-through format that you can implement. (3N, 3L)

INDIVIDUAL LEADERSHIP ACTION PLAN

In each chapter you are asked to create an individual leadership action plan for yourself based on the knowledge and activities that you have learned about. Review your self-assessment results and the "Growing with Intentionality" section and determine some goals that you will establish.

As a result of reading this chapter, I will take the following actions:

I will improve _____ [specific and measurable item] by _____ [what activities will be used to succeed] by _____ [when]. I will assess my growth by _____ [what type of measurement will be used].

I will improve _____ [specific and measurable item] by _____ [what activities will be used to succeed] by _____ [when]. I will assess my growth by _____ [what type of measurement will be used].

EXERCISE 4.1

Consider how effectively the resources of your school community are aligned with the school vision, goals, and roles.

Table 4.1. Resource Alignment

Financial	Budget Allocations
Physical Environment	Safety Plans
	Facility Walk-through Audit
Time	Professional Development Days
	Faculty Meetings
	Team/Department Meetings
Personnel	Meetings
	Supervision and Evaluation

EXERCISE 4.2: MANAGEMENT AND CHANGE FOUR SQUARE

Management of Change: School Initiatives

Part 1: Identify an initiative in your school. List in each square how this meets the four areas of management as reflected in leadership standard 3.

Part 2: Add to each square what additional resources are needed for this initiative to be successful.

Note: This activity could be conducted as a group using large poster paper. (Consider stating, "Identify an initiative in your school. List in each square how these management features are being used. For example, 'We have planning time set aside each week to plan intervention strategies,' or 'We have hired additional personnel through Title I funds to create smaller intervention groups.'")

Time	Personnel
Space: Schedule or Facility	Funding

EXERCISE 4.3: "FITNESS WALKS"

What is a fitness walk (Servais & Sanders, 2006, p. 111)? Fitness walks examine how inviting the school appears to its diverse community. They look at strategies that can be employed to make the school more inviting to the families and community. Fitness walks provide opportunities for parent involvement. They also allow opportunities to improve instructional techniques and curriculum implementation.

Who might benefit: principals, assistant principals, team leaders, teachers, special education teachers, student teachers, parents, and community members.

Purposes for a Fitness Walk

___ Student(s) observation   ___ Classroom event
___ Classroom management   ___ New instructional initiative
___ Curriculum implementation   ___ Daily contacts
___ School culture   ___ Maintenance issues
___ Safe environment   ___ Addressing individual needs

Fitness Walk Protocol

1. Identify the purpose(s) of a fitness walk.
2. Discuss the purpose with classroom teachers whose classrooms you will visit.
3. Develop a method for taking notes during the fitness walk.
4. Write up your observations as soon as possible following the fitness walk.
   a. What did you learn from the fitness walk?
   b. How will the knowledge that you gained from the fitness walk benefit the organization?
   c. How will you disseminate this information to other members of the school community?

LEADERSHIP TOOLS AND RESOURCES FOR GROWTH

Collaborative for Academic, Social, and Emotional Learning:
http://casel.org

Meeting management website:
www.effectivemeetings.com

National School Climate Center:
www.schoolclimate.org/climate

Illinois Children's Mental Health Partnership:
http://icmhp.org/aboutus/aboutmission.html

Social/Emotional Learning standards; Illinois State Board of Education:
www.isbe.state.il.us/ils/social_emotional/standards.htm

National School Safety Center:
www.schoolsafety.us

5

PARTNERSHIPS
Growing Sustainable Relationships

Alone we can do so little; together we can do so much.

—Helen Keller

ISLLC STANDARD 4

Education leaders ensure the success of all students by collaborating with families and stakeholders who represent diverse community interests and needs and by mobilizing community resources that improve teaching and learning.

Standard 4 Summary

In order to educate students effectively for participation in a diverse, democratic society, leaders incorporate participation and views of families and stakeholders for important decisions and activities of schools and districts. Key stakeholders include educators, students, community members, and organizations that serve families and children.

Leaders recognize that diversity enriches and strengthens the education system and a participatory democracy. Leaders regard diverse communities as a resource and work to engage all members in collaboration and partnerships that support teaching and learning. Leaders help teachers communicate positively with families and make sure families understand how to support their children's learning. In communicating with parents and the community, leaders invite feedback and questions so that communities can be partners in providing the best education for every student. (Council of Chief State School Officers, 2008, p. 22)

 ## LEARNING WITH INTENTIONALITY

Collaboration, relationship building, and partnerships are key words in the vocabulary of every effective leader. This chapter examines standard 4 and the complex definitions surrounding what appears to be a relatively simple concept: partnerships. Partnerships might be described as collaborative behavior that results in positive outcomes beneficial to all those involved. A good example of simplified partnerships is to observe two children on a teeter totter. To be successful in this activity, each child must play a part. It is most enjoyed when the leverage is equal, thus making it pleasurable to both participants. While either side can influence the pace and even bring the experience to a stop, this does not benefit either partner. This chapter features ways in which school and district leaders can develop, sustain, and improve by working together as partners. Much like the unspoken rules of a playground, collaboration can provide a mutually beneficial experience for all.

Collaboration is among the terms used most extensively when describing partnerships. But what is it we are describing when we use a term like collaboration? Hank Rubin (2002) defines collaboration as strategic relationships involving one individual at a time to accomplish a shared outcome. The leader has a significant influence in the collaboration between individuals and among the members of the community. The school leader brings together the resources of schools, family members, and the community to positively affect student and adult learning. The school leader seeks out and collaborates with community agencies for health, social, emotional, and other services to families and children.

Leadership is a relationship. According to experts James Kouzes and Barry Posner, leadership is not a single role but rather everyone's business. It is not a position, a place, or a cryptic set of rules. Leadership is building and connecting relationships (Kouzes & Posner, 2006). The collaborative leader commits time and energy in

running the maze of interpersonal and interinstitutional politics that are necessary to build and sustain the interest and involvement of each collaborative partner. Assuming it is in the best interest of the mission to have many partners, the collaborative leader sets out to find a best way to help each individual partner understand and sustain a personal connection with the work of the collaboration by attaching that work to each partner's individual or institutional self interests. (Rubin, 2002, p. 14)

And while great value is placed on collaborative leadership, like many other skills, it must be learned, practiced, and demonstrated. This collaboration results in cultural competence in sharing responsibilities with communities to improve teaching and learning and the development of beneficial relationships with community resources.

Leaders not only build but must also manage partnerships. The formula for relational management looks like this: effective leaders collaborate to build relationships and connect partners; plus, they capitalize on diversity as an asset, which equals strengthened educational programs. Leaders can find support for partnership development and management through the work of the four following resources: Joyce Epstein and colleagues' framework of six roles of parents in school, *School, Family, and Community Partnership: Your Handbook for Action* (2002); Richard DuFour and colleagues' *Learning by Doing: A Handbook for Professional Learning Communities at Work* (2006); Kouzes and Posner's *Encouraging the Heart* (2003); and the Holmes Group's school-university partnership development.

The standard 4 dispositions provide leaders with a well-defined framework and actions for building partnerships. The effective leader shares responsibility to achieve common goals together as partners. A successful school community recognizes the family and community as valued partners and treats them accordingly. Family structures, including cultural, socioeconomic, and ethnic diversity, must be understood and respected more now than ever in America's rapidly changing society. Many of the issues addressed throughout this leadership manual regarding social justice serve as critical knowledge needed for leaders to respect the diverse family structure. Leaders must attempt to mobilize resources to and through the community in ways that result in a win-win situation for students, parents, and the community. Finally, leaders must demonstrate continuous and relentless learning and improvement for all. In the long run, diversity within a community can either strengthen or diminish learning for all.

HIGH STANDARDS FOR ALL

High expectations yield high levels of performance. An old adage suggests that what we expect is what we will get. Consider the Pygmalion effect among the human relation lessons needed for a successful collaborative leader. The Pygmalion effect was illustrated by George Bernard Shaw in *My Fair Lady* through the lead character, Eliza Doolittle. Eliza is a poor and unsophisticated woman whose transformation to a "proper lady" was totally unexpected. Basically, the concept that has evolved from the term "Pygmalion" is that expectations of people and their expectations of themselves are key factors in how well people perform at work and in life. The higher the expectation of performance, the better a person will perform. This self-fulfilling prophecy is not a new concept to education, but it is too often a forgotten one. In other words, members of a school community will evolve to the extent that we expect. Keep in mind that high-performance teachers are often the result of high expectations by the school leader. Likewise, if the role of parents is viewed as equally essential to a child's education, they will contribute as equal partners. Finally, consider a school or school district that operates with high expectations of its community. The natural result will be a community that participates as vital high-performing partners. Standard 4 reminds leaders that they need to hold high expectations for students, faculty, and the community.

Continuous learning requires effective communication and collaboration strategies among faculty, family, and local community partners. The effective leader brings together all the resources of the school, family members, and the community to positively affect student and adult learning. Kouzes and Posner provide a framework as a means for leaders to ensure continuous learning and improvement for all. This framework includes five components from *The Leadership Challenge* (2002) to guide leaders in providing continuous learning and support for the school community. Leaders are encouraged to demonstrate the following five behaviors:

1. Model the way: modeling means going first, living the behaviors you want others to adopt. This is leading from the front. People

will believe not what they hear leaders say but what they see leaders consistently do.

2. Inspire a shared vision: people are motivated not by fear or reward but by ideas that capture their imagination. It is not about having a vision but about communicating it so effectively that others take it as their own.

3. Challenge the process: leaders learn and grow from challenges and adverse situations. They are early adopters of innovation.

4. Enable others to act: empower people to put their ideas into action.

5. Encourage the heart: people perform best when they are passionate about what they are doing. (Encouraging the heart is explored in greater detail in chapter 9, "Celebrating with Intentionality.")

Historically, leaders were successful in a traditional, single, and isolated administrative role to carry out the responsibilities of a school. However, the *Lone Ranger* leadership approach has been replaced by distributive and collaborative models of leadership that rely on the sharing of leadership roles. One of these examples is the Joseph Raelin (2003) model, which identifies four competencies that increase leadership capacity and organizational success: collaborative, collective, concurrent, and compassionate. The paradigm shift, from an authoritarian leader with a single voice to one who will share leadership, requires a very different leadership approach. The Raelin model calls for "shared participation in leadership and decision making at all levels and in multiple decision processes for its members" (Raelin, 2003, p. 76). Shared roles and responsibilities promote reciprocal learning and build leadership within a community or a district office. Formal leadership titles exist but are less evident in a culture where tasks are divided and decisions are made collectively. The Raelin model provides a framework to increase leadership among all partners through distributive and collective leadership and improves the likelihood for success for all stakeholders in a community.

The ultimate partnership, according to the executive council and board of directors of the National Association for Professional Development Schools, may be the school-university partnership, or professional development schools (www.napds.org). The professional development school (PDS) has emerged as a part of the nation's educational partnership alternatives over the past several decades. Unique and particularly intense, school-university collaborations are designed to address four areas: preparing future educators, providing current educators with ongoing professional development, encouraging joint school-university faculty investigation of education-related issues, and promoting the learning of preK–12 students. Essentially, the literature is filled with the benefits of schools and universities sharing resources, personnel, and professional development. However, this symbiotic relationship has been underdeveloped. In spite of the benefits, many schools in need of additional resources have not established partnerships with local colleges or universities.

The school-university partnership provides schools and districts with partners at the university level. For decades, educational experts such as John Goodlad and the Holmes Group have been advocating for an even greater quality of the school-university partners known as professional development schools. At the most basic level, a district or school may collaborate with a university in placing pre-service and student teachers in classrooms. In addition, school and university partners may provide professional development to the school from university faculty, co-write grants, share facilities, and provide other resources. The most extensive partnerships may grow into what is described as a professional development school. Although this term has been used synonymously with partnership schools, it is a much further developed and formal level of collaboration, often based on years of partnership and shared commitments. According to the National Association for Professional Development Schools, there are nine areas that distinguish the PDS:

1. A comprehensive mission that is broader in its outreach and scope than the mission of any partner and that furthers the education profession and its responsibility to advance equity within schools and, by potential extension, the broader community.
2. A school-university culture committed to the preparation of future educators that embraces their active engagement in the school community.
3. Ongoing and reciprocal professional development for all participants guided by need.
4. A shared commitment to innovative and reflective practice by all participants.
5. Engagement in and public sharing of the results of deliberate investigations of practice by respective participants.

6. An articulation agreement developed by the respective participants delineating the roles and responsibilities of all involved.
7. A structure that allows all participants a forum for ongoing governance, reflection, and collaboration.
8. Work by college/university faculty and preK–12 faculty in formal roles across institutional settings.
9. Dedicated and shared resources and formal rewards and recognition structures.

Although many schools may not achieve the formal and comprehensive benefits of a PDS, it is only reasonable to suggest that school leaders and university professors would be wise to intentionally develop school-university partnerships. In some states, such as Illinois, principal preparation programs are required to formalize partnerships with school districts. With efforts to reach out to one another and improve teaching and learning for all participants, the potential economic and educational benefits of partnership schools can become a reality. The school leader who facilitates the school-university partnership gains a valuable resource to benefit preK–12 students. In return, the university provides future teacher and leadership candidates for the next generation.

INCLUDING FAMILY AND COMMUNITY AS PARTNERS

The role of parents in education is unequivocally clear: student success increases when parents are active school partners. Joyce Epstein is among the many educators who have provided decades of work substantiating the role of school, family, and community as partners. Epstein and five coauthors published such a handbook, titled *School, Family, and Community Partnership: Your Handbook for Action* (2002). This valuable resource for leaders provides a framework of six ways that schools can build and sustain successful relationships with parents:

- *Parenting:* Assisting families with parenting and child-rearing skills, and assisting schools in understanding their families.

- *Communicating:* Developing effective communication from home to school and school to home.
- *Volunteering:* Creating ways that families can be involved in the school or school programs and effective methods of recruitment.
- *Learning at home:* Linking families with their children's curriculum through learning activities that can be done at home, as well as homework.
- *Decision-making:* Including families as decision-makers, advocates, members of school councils, and committees.
- *Collaborating with the community:* Coordinating services in the community with family needs and providing services to the community.

The National Network of Partnership Schools (1997) endorses Epstein's framework as a way to help educators develop programs that promote family and community partnerships.

One of the key factors in partnership development is communication. If educators are not able to communicate honestly and effectively, all good intentions of building partners with shared commitments will fall short. The following are five partnership tips that provide leaders, teachers, parents, and university professors with a means for assessment:

- Model honest and productive communication skills.
- Ask more questions than we answer.
- Attentively work to ensure all partners participate in key discussions.
- Note and address nonparticipation.
- Do not permit decisions to be made by implicit endorsements but rather by making sure that each partner is engaged in the decision with an least an active voice, vote, or affirmation of support. (Rubin, 2002)

Leaders need to help teachers communicate positively with families and provide ways for families to support their children's learning. Professors in principal preparation programs likewise have an opportunity to instruct their students about effective communication skills necessary for future principals to work successfully with parents. Professors and leadership mentors have a responsibility to model and teach effective communication skills to future leaders.

Respect for the Diversity of Family Composition

The family structure has undergone many changes over the past two decades. Changes in demographics, urbanization, poverty, and migration have resulted in diverse family compositions, more than at any other time in our society. Family compositions today may be influenced by teenage single parents, divorce, step-families, gay and lesbian parents, and children with special needs. Education and leadership preparation programs have a responsibility to prepare the next generation of teachers and administrators with the skills to understand and respond to diverse families. One resource that provides knowledge in this area of preparation is *Knowing and Serving Diverse Families* by Verna Hildebrand, Lillian A. Phenice, Mary M. Gray, and Rebecca P. Hines (2007). Another resource for school administrators is *Best Leadership Practices for High-Poverty Schools* by Linda L. Lyman and Christine J. Villani (2004). This second resource is recommended as a book talk for high-poverty schools and a standard text for leadership candidates in educational leadership and administration programs. The powerful role parents and teachers can play together is also showcased in a resource called *Creating Welcoming Schools: A Practical Guide to Home-School Partnerships with Diverse Families* by Jo Beth Allen (2007).

Leaders must understand and accommodate diverse students, families, and community conditions. Changing demographics have resulted in parents being more dependent on assistance from third parties, such as school and community agencies. Leaders must be able to demonstrate and assess cultural competency within a school community to meet the diverse needs of students and families. We will provide more on promoting cultural proficiency in chapter 6.

School leaders face a paradoxical challenge of commitment and frustration as they attempt partnership development. There is a high price tag of time and investment for the busy leader to build partnerships; some may be lucrative investments while many may not. One other important caveat to consider is the personality and dispositions of the school leader. While some school leaders will naturally demonstrate standard 4 (promote the success of every student by collaborating with faculty and community members), for other leaders it will be a tremendous challenge. Increasing partnership capacity is a reality that must be valued and developed regardless of a leader's comfort level or collaborative style. Without partnerships, the learning community will most likely fall short. Administrative preparation programs and professional development for educators must include training that prepares future leaders with strategies to build and sustain partnerships for the next generation. Simply put, there is too much to be done to do it alone.

 CARING WITH INTENTIONALITY

Take a moment to read the following dispositions and determine a rating for yourself. We challenge you to not only believe strongly in the following dispositions but also take action in what you believe is important.

Dispositions Exemplified in Standard 4

5	4	3	2	1	0
Highly skilled	Proficient	Average	Limited	Little	No skill

The education leader believes in, values, and is committed to . . .

_____ high standards for all
_____ including family and community as partners
_____ respect for the diversity of family composition
_____ continuous learning and improvements for all

 ASSESSING WITH INTENTIONALITY

Directions

Rate the following items for each standard, with 5 as the highest level of skill ranging to 0 as no skill. Consider your present position and years of leadership experience as you self-assess your performance below. At the end of each standard, reflect on and identify your strengths and challenges, including a final checkup at the conclusion. Your initial preassessment gives you a baseline on your current leadership performance. Once you have completed the exercises provided in *The Courage to Grow*, return to this self-assessment, and retake it to measure your leadership growth.

5	4	3	2	1	0
Highly skilled	Proficient	Average	Limited	Little	No skill

Standard 4: Collaborating with Families and Stakeholders

Education leaders ensure the success of all students by collaborating with families and stakeholders who represent diverse community interests and needs and mobilizing community resources that improve teaching and learning.

Leadership Performance Indicators

Element A: Collaboration with Families and Community Members

A leader . . .

Pre   Post

____ ____ brings together the resources of schools, family members, and community to positively affect student and adult learning, including parents and others who provide care for children. (4A)

____ ____ involves families in decision-making about their children's education. (4B)

____ ____ uses effective public information strategies to communicate with families and community members (such as e-mail, night meetings, and written materials in multiple languages). (4C)

____ ____ applies communication and collaboration strategies to develop family and local community partnerships. (4D)

____ ____ develops comprehensive strategies for positive community and media relations. (4E)

Element B: Community Interests and Needs

A leader . . .

____ ____ identifies key stakeholders and is actively involved within the community, including working with community members and groups that have competing or conflicting perspectives about education. (4F)

_____ _____ uses appropriate assessment strategies and research methods to understand and accommodate diverse student and community conditions and dynamics. (4G)

_____ _____ seeks out and collaborates with community programs serving students with special needs. (4H)

_____ _____ capitalizes on diversity (such as cultural, ethnic, racial, economic, and special interest groups) as an asset of the school community to strengthen educational programs. (4I)

_____ _____ demonstrates cultural competence in sharing responsibilities with communities to improve teaching and learning. (4J)

Element C: Building on Community Resources to Maximize Shared Resources

A leader . . .

_____ _____ links to and collaborates with community agencies for health, social, and other services to families and children. (4K)

_____ _____ develops mutually beneficial relationships with business, religious, political, and service organizations to share school and community resources (such as buildings, playing fields, parks, medical clinics, and so on). (4L)

_____ _____ uses public resources and funds appropriately and effectively. (4M)

_____ _____ secures community support to sustain existing resources and add new resources that address emerging student needs. (4N)

_____ _____ Standard 4 Total

Standard 4 Leadership Attributes

Personal Strengths:

_____

_____

_____

Personal Challenges:

_____

_____

_____

GROWING WITH INTENTIONALITY: LEADING THROUGH PARTNERSHIPS

In order to strengthen your competencies, based on your particular leadership role, review the following exercises. Using the results of your assessment, choose an exercise or two and then write them into the SMART goal format located at the end of this section.

District- and School-Level Administrators

- Create a public comment area on the district's website to allow parents and community members to share their thoughts and opinions in an open forum. Have district personnel review the public's insight on an ongoing basis so that the public understands you are there to serve them and their children. (4B, 4C, 4E)
- Contact your area college or university, and determine ways that they can be a resource for your school or district (e.g., staff development presentations, leadership development workshops, future teachers and leaders as interns, additional assistance in classrooms, or discounted courses for teachers and leaders). (4F, 4K, 4L)
- Review the partnership websites listed at the end of this chapter. Identify three to five partnership practices that would benefit your school or district, and create a plan to begin these practices. (4D, 4G, 4N)
- Interview several parents to gather their insights on curriculum, school improvement goals, grading practices, communication, and the role of parents as partners. This will provide you with more in-depth insights into the needs of stakeholders. (4F, 4H, 4I)
- Examine your present parent-teacher conference procedures. Identify ways to increase parent participation. Identify popula-

tion issues that may cause parents not to attend (e.g., language issues, low socioeconomic issues). (4B, 4J)

• Analyze strengths and weaknesses of student-led conferences. (4B)

Professors in Educational Administration Programs

• Ask your students to interview a few parents from their district about how they would like to become more involved in the school community. This could be an easy survey of only a few questions. Examples: In what ways have you been involved in the school communities that your children attend? Would you have liked to be more involved in the decisions that were made at your child's school? If so, how? What have been some challenges you have faced in being more involved in the school community? What can the schools do to get more parents involved in their children's education? (4F, 4H, 4I)

• Assign your students to interview several parents to gather their perspectives on curriculum, school improvement goals, grading practices, communication, and the role of parents as partners. This will provide you with more in-depth insights into the needs of stakeholders. (4F, 4H, 4I)

• Have your students analyze student-led conferences to determine the strengths and weaknesses within their educational organizations. (4B)

Leadership Candidates and Teacher Leaders

• With budgetary deficits at the forefront of most districts, teacher leaders and educational administration candidates should create a list of local businesses that the school can partner with to mutually support one another. For instance, you can help your administrators set up an assembly on Internet safety by calling your local law enforcement agencies or asking a local lawyer to come in and share their knowledge, free of charge. You can also ask the fire department to come in and share information on fire safety. These relationships are important to show your students that local community agencies assist one another. (4A, 4K, 4M)

• Assist your administrator in surveying parents within your school setting by asking some of the following questions: In what ways have you been involved in the school communities that your children attend? Would you have liked to be more involved in the decisions that were made at your child's school? If so, how? What have been some challenges you have faced in being more involved in the school community? What can the schools do to get more parents involved in their children's education? (4F, 4H, 4I)

- Attend your local school board meetings to get a better idea of what is going on in the community. Keep notes of the major issues that are addressed at the meetings, and see how that information relates to establishing and sustaining strong partnerships with all stakeholders. (4D, 4F, 4L)
- Interview several parents to gather their perspectives on curriculum, school improvement goals, grading practices, communication, and the role of parents as partners. This will provide you with more in-depth insights into the needs of stakeholders. (4F, 4H, 4I)
- Examine your present parent-teacher conference procedures. Identify ways to increase parent participation. Identify issues that may cause parents not to attend (e.g., language issues, low socioeconomic issues). (4B, 4J)
- Analyze the strengths and weaknesses of student-led conferences. (4B)

INDIVIDUAL LEADERSHIP ACTION PLAN

In each chapter you are asked to create an individual leadership action plan for yourself based on the knowledge and activities that you have learned about. Review your self-assessment results and the "Growing with Intentionality" section, and determine some goals that you will establish.

As a result of reading this chapter, I will take the following actions:

I will improve _____ [specific and measurable item] by _____ [what strategies will be used to succeed] by _____ [when]. I will assess my growth by _____ [what type of measurement will be used].

I will improve _____ [specific and measurable item] by _____ [what strategies will be used to succeed] by _____ [when]. I will assess my growth by _____ [what type of measurement will be used].

EXERCISE 5.1

The National Parent Teacher Association (1990) has developed the following questionnaire to determine if families feel welcome in a school.

How Welcome Are Parents in Our School?

Directions

Think about the experiences you have had when you have visited your child's school. Please take a few minutes to fill out the following brief survey. Be honest. The results of this survey will be analyzed to determine recommendations that may be necessary to help you, our parents, feel more welcome in our school.

1. Am I always greeted in a friendly, courteous way when I contact the school either on the phone or in person? Yes ___ No___
2. Does the school have a reception area for visitors that is equipped with information about the school and directions so that I can find my way around the building? Yes___ No___
3. Did the school conduct some kind of orientation program for my family when I first enrolled my child? Yes___ No___
4. Do school staff members and parents have informal occasions when we can get to know each other during the school year? Yes___ No___
5. Does the principal have regular office hours when parents and students can stop in? Yes___ No___
   Note: If "yes" to the above question, are those hours convenient for me?
6. Is there a school suggestion box where teachers', students', and parents' ideas are encouraged, and are ideas implemented when possible? Yes___ No___

7. Does the school encourage me to visit my child's classroom outside of planned occasions (after checking first with the teacher involved)? Yes___ No___
8. Am I and other parents welcome to use the building after school hours for community purposes? Yes___ No___
9. Does the principal ask for parents' suggestions when making decisions that will affect the running of the school? Yes___ No___
10. Are limited-English-speaking parents given opportunities to understand the curriculum and participate in the school's activities? Yes___ No___
11. Does the school provide written information to parents about school rules, parent-teacher conferences, and other important items? Yes___ No___

Review your responses. How satisfied are you with your school and the role of parents? What recommendations would you make to your school to create a more inclusive environment for parents?

LEADERSHIP TOOLS AND RESOURCES FOR GROWTH

"What It Means to Be a Professional Development School—A Statement by the Executive Council and Board of Directors of the National Association for Professional Development Schools": www.napds.org/9%20Essentials/statement.pdf

Center on School, Family, and Community Partnerships: www.csos.jhu.edu/p2000/center.htm

National Coalition for Parent Involvement in Education: www.ncpie.org

6

LEADERSHIP ETHICS AND INTEGRITY
A Code of Conduct for All

To care for anyone else enough to make their problems one's own, is ever the beginning of one's real ethical development.

—Felix Adler

ISLLC STANDARD 5

Education leaders ensure the success of all students by being ethical and acting with integrity.

Standard 5 Summary

Local and state education agencies and professional organizations hold educators to codes of ethics, with attention to personal conduct, fiscal responsibilities, and other types of ethical requirements. The Performance Expectations build on concepts of professional ethics and integrity and add an emphasis on responsibilities of leaders for educational equity and social justice in a democratic society. Education is the primary socializing institution, conferring unique benefits or deficits across diverse constituents.

Leaders recognize that there are existing inequities in current distribution of high-quality educational resources among students. Leaders remove barriers to high-quality education that derive from economic, social, cultural, linguistic, physical, gender, or other sources of discrimination and disadvantage. They hold high expectations of every student and [ensure] that all students have what they need to learn what is expected. Further, leaders are responsible for distributing the unique benefits of education more equitably, expanding future opportunities of less-advantaged students and families and increasing social justice across a highly diverse population.

Current policy environments with high-stakes accountability in education require that leaders are responsible for positive and negative consequences of their interpretations and implementation of policies as they affect students, educators, communities, and their own positions. Politically skilled, well-informed leaders understand and negotiate complex policies (such as high-stakes accountability), avoiding potential harm to students, educators, or communities that result from ineffective or insufficient approaches.

Ethics and integrity mean leading from a position of caring, modeling care and belonging in educational settings, personally in their behavior and professionally in concern about students, their learning, and their lives. Leaders demonstrate and sustain a culture of trust, openness, and reflection about values and beliefs in education. They model openness about how to improve learning of every student. They engage others to share decisions and monitor consequences of decisions and actions on students, educators, and communities. (Council of Chief State School Officers, 2008, p. 25)

 LEARNING WITH INTENTIONALITY

The fifth standard highlights the importance of being ethical and acting with integrity. The key issues in the area of ethics and integrity are social justice, diversity and equity, cultural proficiency, and personal and organizational values and beliefs. Current and future leaders need to create a personal and professional code of conduct to address these key issues: "As educators, we can no longer ignore the needs of these (our diverse) students. Our moral integrity is at risk when . . . we wait to see what the next mandate will be from the state house rather than teach in ways that are culturally responsive" (Lindsey, Martinez, & Lindsey, 2007, p. 7). Ethically, we need to teach students what they need in order to be successful and not just to meet the mandates of the state or federal government. In this chapter, we share knowledge of social justice, diversity and equity, cultural proficiency, and personal and organizational values and beliefs, and then provide examples of activities to strengthen these areas within your educational environment.

CONTINUOUSLY IMPROVING KNOWLEDGE AND SKILLS: SOCIAL JUSTICE

What is meant by social justice? Social justice is defined as a society or institution based on the principles of equality that values human rights and that recognizes the dignity of every human being. In other words, social justice exists as the foundation to all educational actions and decisions. Helen Keller stated that "until the great mass of the people shall be filled with the sense of responsibility for each other's welfare, social justice can never be attained." That belief is more fundamental than ever in guaranteeing the rights and welfare of all children. Decisions that are made at each level of education should consider the impact that these decisions have on the human rights of all students. The reauthorization of the Elementary and Secondary Education Act (ESEA) of 2001, commonly referred to as No Child Left Behind (NCLB), provides a lens with an equitable view of all students regardless of race, ethnicity, social class, language skills, and learning abilities. While this controversial law has not been without criticism, it has engaged educators in a process to identify and disaggregate data to be certain that no students are left behind.

Leaders must be able to embrace ethics as a critical focus in educational decisions to make certain the principles of social justice are achieved for all. Principal preparation programs have a responsibility to forecast the difficult ethical decisions leaders must make and help future leaders to determine an awareness of values they must possess on behalf of all students. Equally vital is the role of the superintendent in a school district to model advocacy and social justice for all students even in difficult situations. Joseph Zajda states, "Ethics must be the core of social justice in teacher preparation and the formation of new leaders in education. Central to this vision is the fact that social justice is fundamentally a call to transformative actions needed to advance equity, equitable access to education, freedom from discrimination, and the principles of a democratic society" (2009, p. 4). Educators need to use the barometer of social justice when selecting curricular materials, spending resources, hiring staff, involving stakeholders, changing district boundaries, utilizing grant dollars, reviewing instructional practices, and making all other decisions that impact the rights of students. This may be a cultural challenge for nondiverse schools where issues of social justice have not been brought to the forefront in the daily operations and decisions regarding students. The effective leader recognizes this challenge and identifies processes in decision-making that demonstrate respect for the inherent dignity and worth of each individual.

THE COMMON GOOD OVER PERSONAL INTERESTS: DIVERSITY AND EQUITY

It is impossible to talk about educators being ethical and acting with integrity without discussing diversity and equity. In our global society, many people are still denied the right to an education based on their race, ethnicity, religion, or gender. In the United States, there is a perception that there have been great gains in providing a high-quality education for all without regard to demographics. However, leaders in high-need schools may argue this point as they continue to battle inadequate educational conditions. Linda Darling-Hammond writes that it is time to "make good on the unmet American promise that education will be made available to all on equal terms, so that every member of this society can realize a productive life and contribute to the greater welfare" (2010, p. 3). What does this mean for leaders? The effective leader models personal and professional ethics, integrity, justice, and fairness and expects the same of others.

Many school districts are initiating diversity audits to ensure they are addressing the issues of diversity and equity. One district that has conducted such an audit is in the suburbs of Chicago. The audit was conducted by a diversity consulting group, and it was designed to conduct interviews with focus groups made up of staff members, students, parents, and community members from various races and ethnicities. The groups were homogeneous and allowed for more honest and open dialogue. The data from this particular audit highlighted four areas that the district needed to address in order to be more effective. These four focus areas were as follows: to provide better communication tools to keep all community informed in a timely manner; to provide better advancement opportunities for people from diverse races and ethnicities; to seek better employment strategies to increase minority representation in all levels within the district; and to create and implement a plan to address racial or ethnic controversies that have occurred or may occur in the future. The results of such an audit can provide valuable data to study and improve equity within a community.

Effective districts and schools are responsive to the diverse needs of their communities. A district equity advisory council was created in this suburban district to address the four focus areas and to guide the district to be more proactive than reactive. The council would meet monthly to discuss actions that could be taken to provide more intentional staff development for teachers and leaders as well as to determine impactful social-emotional learning opportunities that could be offered to the students at all levels. It also allows districts to be very transparent in their approaches to these issues so that the community understands the expectations of the diversity and equity plan.

ETHICAL PRINCIPLES IN ALL RELATIONSHIPS AND DECISIONS

Another ethics issue associated with diversity and equity is how the district creates, implements, and assesses curriculum. In the same vein as social justice, it is imperative for districts to align their curriculum to meet the needs of all students. For instance, if you work in a district that has a high Latino population, you want to ensure that the resources are available not only in Spanish but also in stories that are of interest to the Latino students. Curricular resources need to be purchased and distributed in an equitable manner to address all the demographic student needs of the district. Many schools have very differing needs even within one district, and it is vital that districts consider the diverse needs of each school and make resource allocation accordingly. For example, if all schools have equal amounts of technology, this does not take into consideration students from low-income families who may not have access to technology at home and need to have more technology opportunities at school (as opposed to a school that has more affluent families). Leaders must make decisions in schools and districts by first looking through the lens of diversity and equity to ensure they are acting with integrity and in an ethical manner for all.

CULTURAL PROFICIENCY

In order to impact a school and district, leaders must find ways to improve cultural proficiency for each stakeholder: "Cultural proficiency is a lens through which we frame our personal and organizational learning and develop principles to guide our personal behaviors and organizational policies and practices" (Lindsey, Jungwirth, Pahl, & Lindsey, 2009, p. 7). Teachers, administrators, professors, and school partners must assess their own assumptions and values regarding academic achievement for students who have traditionally been underserved and be given opportunities to dialogue about ways to respect the differences and dignity. The effective leader respectfully challenges and works to change assumptions and beliefs that negatively affect students, educational environments, and student learning. Professional development provides opportunities to discuss ways to overcome barriers, resistance to change, and ways to develop a more inclusive cultural environment (Lindsey, Jungwirth, Pahl, & Lindsey, 2009). Figure 6.1 is taken from the resource *Culturally Proficient Learning Communities* (2009) and showcases a growth chart and discussion to improve cultural proficiency.

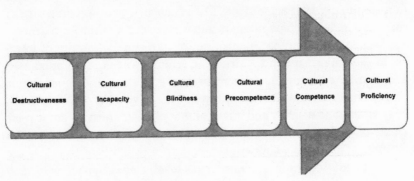

Figure 6.1.   Path to Cultural Proficiency

▶ *Cultural destructiveness:* In what areas in your educational environment are people seeking to eliminate other cultures or cultural values?

_____

_____

_____

▶ *Cultural incapacity:* Are there people in your organization that lead in a way that trivializes other cultures and seek to make the culture of others appear to be wrong? What do you think can be done to move these people to become more culturally proficient?

_____

_____

_____

▶ *Cultural blindness:* Do you know anyone within your organization who leads in a manner where they don't see or acknowledge the culture of others and may choose to ignore the discrepant experiences of cultures within the school or district? How can these people be moved toward a more culturally proficient leadership?

_____

_____

_____

▶ *Cultural precompetence:* Often we need to be made aware of what we don't know about diversity before we can lead sustainable change. How have you or others within your organization led with an increased awareness of what you don't know about working in diverse settings?

_____

_____

_____

▶ *Cultural competence:* In what ways do you lead with alignment of your personal values and behaviors with the school's policies and practices? This alignment should be demonstrated in a manner that is inclusive of cultures that are new or different from you and the school or district.

_____

_____

_____

▶ *Cultural proficiency:* Give an example of a time that you or a leader within your organization led as an advocate for lifelong learning with the purpose of being increasingly effective in serving the educational needs of cultural groups.

_____

_____

_____

(Lindsey, Jungwirth, Pahl, & Lindsey, 2009)

One way leaders can provide staff development to increase cultural proficiency is to conduct a book study on the topic of diversity and equity. At one elementary school, the entire staff participated in a book study on *Courageous Conversations about Race: A Field Guide for Achieving Equity in Schools* (Singleton & Linton, 2006). This book study was formatted so that teams of teachers would read a particular chapter and then facilitate a learning session for their peers. This allowed everyone to learn about different perspectives on cultural proficiency. An interesting outcome of this book study was that, even though many teachers were frustrated by the requirement to participate, they all took away new insights about diversity and equity. Many of the learning sessions focused on understanding what our diverse parents, students, and community members desire from educators. The *Courageous Conversations* book study allowed the staff to alter some past practices on how they differentiated instruction to meet the individual needs of the students as well as how they facilitated parent-teacher conferences.

TAKING RESPONSIBILITY FOR ACTIONS: PERSONAL AND ORGANIZATIONAL VALUES AND BELIEFS

In order to act in an ethical manner, leaders need to understand their personal values and beliefs. Leaders should expect some discomfort for themselves and others as they journey through personal and organizational beliefs and values regarding equity: "Minimally, you should be disturbed enough to reflect on your personal values and beliefs and those of your school and district. It should be clear to you the direct link between what you value, what you assume, and how your assumptions shape what you believe to be true. Ultimately, your actions spring from your beliefs of what you assume to be true" (Campbell Jones, Campbell Jones, & Lindsey, 2010, p. 114). Values and beliefs should serve as an ethical compass to direct our actions and decisions that take place within a school or district. If the ethical compass causes us to feel uncomfortable or to question certain actions, then we should change directions, or at least reconsider the direction we are going.

Self-awareness of beliefs and values are essential in promoting cultural proficiency. However, educators rarely discuss or spend time reflecting on how personal and professional values and beliefs impact their actions. In *The Courage to Lead*, we emphasized the importance of identifying, acting, and reflecting on our beliefs. We highlighted activities through which leaders can identify not only their personal beliefs but also how they found that belief or value. Once leaders have identified their personal goals, they need to take action to demonstrate these beliefs to others. For an example of this connection between belief and action, a leader believes that visibility is important in the school and district and so takes action that is visible in buildings and classrooms many times throughout a week. However, oftentimes leaders may find a disconnect between what they value and their actions. For example, a leader believes that communication with all stakeholders is important but then fails to respond to e-mails or phone calls. Exercise 6.1 provides an activity that leaders can use to reflect on their beliefs and actions. This exercise is an opportunity for you to assess the congruence between your beliefs and your actions.

MODELING HIGH EXPECTATIONS

Effective leaders model ethics and values through meaningful professional development expectations. Teachers require time to hold pivotal conversations with peers regarding equity, social justice, and cultural proficiency. Teachers who are isolated and fail to discuss challenging issues with each other will not reach clarity for themselves and others. One way to strengthen these pivotal conversations is to use a conversational format. One approach that has been utilized is called "crucial conversations." In *Crucial Conversations* (Patterson, Grenny, McMillan, & Switzler, 2002), the authors state that this is "a discussion between two people where 1) stakes are high, 2) opinions vary, and 3) emotions run strong" (p. 3). The key elements to having these crucial conversations follow:

1. Clarify what you want and what you don't want to result from conversation.
2. Attempt to find mutual purpose.
3. Create a safe environment for honest dialogue.
4. Use facts.
5. Share your thought process that has led to conversation.
6. Encourage recipients to share their facts and thought processes.

Consider a time when you needed to have a crucial conversation but were reluctant to do so. How would these six tips help you to conduct that important conversation? When discussing issues such as equity, social justice, cultural proficiency, and personal and professional beliefs and values, it is extremely likely that everyone within your organization will have differing views about these issues. The culturally proficient leader is proactive and encourages many opportunities for crucial conversations to occur to better meet the needs of all students.

 CARING WITH INTENTIONALITY

Take a moment to read the following dispositions and determine a rating for yourself. We challenge you to not only believe strongly in the following dispositions but also take action in what you believe is important.

Dispositions Exemplified in Standard 5

5	4	3	2	1	0
Highly skilled	Proficient	Average	Limited	Little	No skill

Education leaders believe in, value, and are committed to . . .

_____ continuously improving knowledge and skills
_____ the common good over personal interests
_____ ethical principles in all relationships and decisions
_____ taking responsibility for actions
_____ modeling high expectations

 ASSESSING WITH INTENTIONALITY

Directions

Rate the following items for each standard, with 5 as the highest level of skill ranging to 0 as no skill. Consider your present position and years of leadership experience as you self-assess your performance below. At the end of each standard, reflect on and identify your strengths and challenges, including a final checkup at the conclusion. Your initial preassessment gives you a baseline on your current leadership performance. Once you have completed the exercises provided in *The Courage to Grow*, return to this self-assessment and retake it to measure your leadership growth.

5	4	3	2	1	0
Highly skilled	Proficient	Average	Limited	Little	No skill

Standard 5: Ethics and Integrity

Education leaders ensure the success of all students by being ethical and acting with integrity.

Leadership Performance Indicators

Element A: Ethical and Legal Standards

A leader . . .

Pre   *Post*

____   ____   models personal and professional ethics, integrity, justice, and fairness and expects the same of others. (5A)

____   ____   protects the rights and appropriate confidentiality of students and staff. (5B)

____   ____   behaves in a trustworthy manner, using professional influence and authority to enhance education and the common good. (5C)

Element B: Examining Personal Values and Beliefs

A leader . . .

____   ____   demonstrates respect for the inherent dignity and worth of each individual. (5D)

____   ____   models respect for diverse community stakeholders and treats them equitably. (5E)

____   ____   demonstrates respect for diversity by developing cultural competency skills and equitable practices. (5F)

____   ____   assesses own personal assumptions, values, beliefs, and practices that guide improvement of student learning. (5G)

____   ____   uses a variety of strategies to lead others in safely examining deeply held assumptions and beliefs that may conflict with vision and goals. (5H)

____   ____   respectfully challenges and works to change assumptions and beliefs that negatively affect students, educational environments, and student learning. (5I)

Element C: Maintaining High Standards for Self and Others

A leader . . .

____   ____   reflects on own work, analyzes strengths and weaknesses, and establishes goals for professional growth. (5J)

_____ _____ models lifelong learning by continually deepening understanding and practice related to content, standards,
assessment, data, teacher support, evaluation, and professional development strategies. (5K)

_____ _____ develops and uses understanding of educational policies
such as accountability to avoid expedient, inequitable,
or unproven approaches that meet short-term goals
(such as raising test scores). (5L)

_____ _____ helps educators and the community understand and
focus on vision and goals for students within political
conflicts over educational purposes and methods. (5M)

_____ _____ sustains personal motivation, optimism, commitment,
energy, and health by balancing professional and personal responsibilities and encouraging similar actions
for others. (5N)

_____ _____ Standard 5 Total

Standard 5 Leadership Attributes

Personal Strengths:

_____

_____

_____

Personal Challenges:

_____

_____

_____

 **GROWING WITH INTENTIONALITY:
LEADERSHIP ETHICS**

In order to strengthen your competencies, based on your particular
leadership role, review the following exercises. Using the results of your

assessment, choose an exercise or two and then write them into the SMART goal format located at the end of this section.

District- and School-Level Administrators

- Develop homogeneous focus groups to discuss issues associated with diversity and equity in the community. Identify questions to engage the participants in a discussion about the issues. Consider using a clock buddy (ELP 8.2) to ask participants to partner with someone else in the community to discuss each of the questions. Share results and postsummary statements of what was learned. (5D, 5E, 5H)
- Identify a time when you found it difficult to conduct a vital conversation. Take the six tips from *Crucial Conversations* and hold a challenging conversation with a peer. You may wish to use this as a practice or mock conversation. Ask a peer to listen and give you feedback. Reverse roles. How will this exercise prepare you for the next crucial conversation you must initiate as a leader? (5H, 5I)
- Introduce and participate in a book study on *Teaching with Poverty in Mind* by Eric Jensen (2009). Utilize the study guide that accompanies this book to discuss and examine the issues of poverty on student achievement. The study guide can be found at www.ascd.org/publications/books/109074/chapters/A-Study-Guide-for-Teaching-with-Poverty-in-Mind@-What-Being-Poor-Does-to-Kids%27-Brains-and-What-Schools-Can-Do-About-It .aspx. (5G, 5I)
- Investigate the social-emotional standards and ways to incorporate these into existing curriculum. Investigate websites such as the Center for Social and Emotional Education at www.school-climate.org/climate; the Illinois State Board at www.isbe.state .il.us/ils/social_emotional/standards.htm; or the Collaborative for Academic, Social, and Emotional Learning (CASEL) at http://casel.org to examine the research and ways social and emotional learning (SEL) can impact learning. Also consider an additional resource such as *Social and Emotional Learning in the Classroom: Promoting Mental Health and Academic Success* (Merrell & Gueldner, 2010). (5I, 5K)
- Have district-level administrators or staff members analyze and assess social justice issues that have occurred in school districts

around the country—for instance, a gay/lesbian couple going to prom as a couple, prayer in schools, sexting, social networking issues that come into the school setting, and other ethical decisions that are addressed in schools. Have the administrators or teachers identify the different sides associated with each issue and what conflicts may arise based on the various decision options. This is a very proactive activity to address some of these issues before they actually occur in your district. (*Crucial Conversations*; 5A, 5B)

- Develop a leadership code of ethics for the district office and school leaders. Work in partners to identify key statements for consideration. Post all of the statements on a large sheet of poster paper. Discuss the implications and ethical behavior related to each. Provide each participant with five sticky dots, and ask each to select the five statements most aligned to their own ethics. Determine the top choices, and repeat the discussion on the implications and commitment to these statements as a code of ethics. Upon completing the activity, have a final copy of the code of ethics printed and laminated for each leader. (5A, 5B, 5C)
- Conduct a discussion on the merits, challenges, and integrity of grading. Utilize resources from Doug Reeves to discuss the research on grading, including a history of toxic grading practices. Materials on this topic (webinars, videos, and articles) can be found at www.leadandlearn.com. View "Effective Grading Practices," by Doug Reeves, as a leadership team, and complete the activities together. Propose several improved grading systems for your district, and attempt to come to consensus on one of the proposals. (5H, 5K, 5L)

Professors in Educational Administration Programs

- Participate in a faculty book study at your college or university on a current diversity issue in leadership preparation. Possible selections are *Courageous Conversations About Race: A Field Guide for Achieving Equity in Schools* (Singleton & Linton, 2006), *Everyday Antiracism: Getting Real About Race in School* (Pollock, 2008), and *Cultural Proficiency: A Manual for School Leaders* (Lindsey, Robins, & Terrell, 2003). (5G, 5I)
- Have students analyze and assess social justice issues that have occurred in school districts around the country—for instance, a

gay/lesbian couple going to prom as a couple, prayer in schools, and other ethical decisions that are addressed in schools. Have the students identify the different perspectives associated with each issue and determine the conflicts that may arise based on potential decisions. (5A, 5B)

- Develop a leadership code of ethics for the educational leadership department. Work in partners to identify key statements for consideration. Post all of the statements on a large sheet of poster paper. Discuss the implications and ethical behavior related to each. Provide each participant with five sticky dots, and ask each to select the five statements most aligned to their own ethics. Determine the top choices, and repeat the discussion on the implications and commitment to these statements as a code of ethics. Upon completing the activity, have a final copy of the code of ethics printed and laminated for each leader. (5A, 5B, 5C)
- Conduct a discussion on the merits, challenges, and integrity of grading. Utilize resources from Doug Reeves to discuss the research on grading, including a history of toxic grading practices. Materials on this topic (webinars, videos, and articles) can be found at www .leadandlearn.com. View "Effective Grading Practices," by Doug Reeves, as a leadership team, and complete the activities together. Propose several improved grading systems and attempt to come to consensus on one of the proposals. (5H, 5K, 5L)

Leadership Candidates and Teacher Leaders

- Join a professional organization as a student and investigate the mission, values, and ethics. (5K, 5N)
- Have someone write a letter of reference for you for an administrative position. Have them highlight various core values and ethics that you demonstrate. (5J)
- Write a letter of interest for a position that you may desire, and highlight your values and ethical strengths. Consider how you demonstrate your ethics and values on a daily basis. (5A, 5J)
- Develop a leadership code of ethics for leadership candidates or teacher leaders in the organization. Work in partners to identify key statements for consideration. Post all of the statements on a large sheet of poster paper. Discuss the implications and

ethical behavior related to each. Provide each participant with five sticky dots, and ask each to select the five statements most aligned to their own ethics. Determine the top choices, and repeat the discussion on the implications and commitment to these statements as a code of ethics. Upon completing the activity, have a final copy of the code of ethics printed and laminated for each leader. (5A, 5B, 5C)

- Conduct a discussion on the merits, challenges, and integrity of grading. Utilize resources from Doug Reeves to discuss the research on grading, including a history of toxic grading practices. Materials on this topic (webinars, videos, and articles) can be found at www .leadandlearn.com. View "Effective Grading Practices," by Doug Reeves, as a leadership team, and complete the activities together. Propose several improved grading systems, and attempt to come to consensus on one of the proposals. (5H, 5K, 5L)

INDIVIDUAL LEADERSHIP ACTION PLAN

In each chapter you are asked to create an individual leadership action plan for yourself based on the knowledge and activities that you have learned about. Review your self-assessment results and the "Growing with Intentionality" section, and determine some goals that you will establish.

As a result of reading this chapter, I will take the following actions:

I will improve _____ [specific and measurable item] by _____ [what strategies will be used to succeed] by _____ [when]. I will assess my growth by _____ [what type of measurement will be used].

I will improve _____ [specific and measurable item] by _____ [what strategies will be used to succeed] by _____ [when]. I will assess my growth by _____ [what type of measurement will be used].

EXERCISE 6.1

Take time to reflect on your beliefs and the actions associated with them. Use this exercise to measure your organization values and beliefs by having various stakeholders respond to the questions to see how well everyone understands what you value and believe as a school or district.

1. How do your beliefs support your actions? What are three of your primary beliefs?

   _____

   _____

   _____

2. Identify specific examples of your daily actions and how these illustrate your beliefs:

   _____

   _____

   _____

3. Identify artifacts or evidence of your leadership beliefs or your organization beliefs (some examples may be school goals, newsletters, bulletins, or notes from stakeholders):

   _____

   _____

   _____

LEADERSHIP TOOLS AND RESOURCES FOR GROWTH

Equity audit ideas:
www.idra.org/IDRA_Newsletter/March_2001_Self_Renewing_
   Schools_Access_Equity_and_Excellence/Coming_of_Age
http://staffdevelopment.ccps.org/pdf/Cultural%20Proficiency%20
   Receptivity%20Scale.pdf

Center for Social and Emotional Education:
www.schoolclimate.org/climate

Leadership and Learning Center:
www.leadandlearn.com

7

THE POLITICS
OF LEADERSHIP
Understanding and Responding
to Political Perspectives

Educational administrators and vocal special-interest groups by controlling the content of standards and test can control the political content of instruction. The result could be a uniformity of political ideas being taught to students which will reduce the diversity of thinking so vital to a democratic society.

—Spring, 2005, p. 113

ISLLC STANDARD 6

Education leaders ensure the success of all students by influencing inter-related systems of political, social, economic, legal, and cultural contexts affecting education to advocate for their teachers' and students' needs.

Standard 6 Summary

Leaders understand that public schools belong to the public and contribute to the public good. They see schools and districts as part of larger local, state, and federal systems that support success of every student, while increasing equity and social justice. Leaders see education as an open system in which policies, goals, resources, and ownership cross traditional ideas about organizational boundaries of schools or districts.

Education leaders advocate for education and students in professional, social, political, economic, and other arenas. They recognize how principles and structures of governance affect federal, state, and local policies and work to influence and interpret changing norms and policies to benefit all students.

Professional relationships with a range of stakeholders and policymakers enable leaders to identify, respond to, and influence issues, public awareness, and policies. For example, local elections affect education boards and bond results, in turn affecting approaches and resources for student success. Educators who participate in the broader system strive to provide information and engage constituents with data to sustain progress and address needs. Education leaders in a variety of roles contribute special skills and insights to the legal, economic, political, and social well-being of educational organizations and environments. (Council of Chief State School Officers, 2008, p. 28)

 ## LEARNING WITH INTENTIONALITY

Historically, the people furthest away from the classroom are the people who are creating educational policies and mandates. The manner in which policies are developed and communicated might remind us of a childhood game called Telephone. Basically, Telephone is a game where one person whispers a phrase to their neighbor in a line and then sees if the same phrase is repeated correctly by the time it reaches the last person. Politics, like the game of Telephone, often results in policies and mandates not accurately implemented at the classroom level because somewhere in the chain of people the directive becomes misconstrued. Standard 6 provides leaders with strategies to communicate effectively with key decision-makers. A competent leader communicates effectively with key decision-makers in the community and in broader political contexts to improve public understanding of laws, policies, regulations, and statutory requirements.

What is needed, however, is a reciprocal accountability relationship in which all stakeholders are responsible for the intellectual growth of students and the success of schooling as an institution. Within such a relationship, those furthest away from the classroom and furthest away from the lowest rung of the current educational system are equally implicated in the failure of schools to leave no child behind. Within such a relationship, education as a public good becomes an ethical responsibility of all and implicates every American as an agent in the battle to leave no child behind. (Easley, 2005, p. 503)

Educational and political leaders need to ensure the success of all students by using their influence to produce effective systems. Leaders should examine educational initiatives through the following filters: advocating for children and education, influencing policies, upholding and improving laws and regulations, eliminating barriers to improvement, and building on diverse social and cultural assets. Leaders can't wait for policies to be created and implemented because, by the time this slow political process is complete, the students most impacted have already moved through the educational system. The lack of urgency results in irreparable harm to our students, educational system, and ultimately our society.

ADVOCATING FOR CHILDREN AND EDUCATION

Every policy or procedure that is created and implemented in the field of education should pass the first political filter, advocate for all children. The professionals in the field of medicine follow the Hippocratic oath, which basically states, "First do no harm." Would it be fitting to apply this same oath to educational policies? Effective leaders go well beyond this oath of "doing no harm" by relentlessly setting and achieving high expectations for their students. Schools historically have been complacent about equity issues and efforts to close the achievement gap. To make matters worse, many school leaders perceive their roles as lacking the authority and time to influence educational policies that have the potential to reduce this gap. The challenge for the school leader is summed up well in indicator 6C: The leader advocates for equity and adequacy in providing for students' and families' educational, physical, emotional, social, cultural, legal, and economic needs, so every student can meet educational expectations and policy goals. The fundamental question remains: What can the school leader do as an advocate for students regarding policy development?

Many educators, in an era of increased standardized testing and federal government mandates, find themselves straying from the original purpose of school to facilitate learning and develop productive citizens.

This movement away from the fundamental purpose is not in the best interest of the public good: "The tension between the politics of education and education as a public good is continually perpetuated through the belief that education has been treated as a new frontier by contemporary political leadership and that growing interest in public education from political figure heads has greatly influenced the ideology around school failure as well as the language of school reform" (Easley, 2005, p. 494). This political tension is not putting the interests of children first but instead is causing a greater divide between schools and society.

In order to advocate for all students, educational leaders must address funding inequities. Leaders must address these inequities "within districts and states; find ways that provide low income/urban students with the intellectual, social, and emotional tools needed to access the broader socio-political and economic structures that exist beyond their home environments, and find ways that address civil liberties for all students regardless of race, class, gender, sexual identity, and ability" (Easley, 2005, p. 503). One way for leaders to find more information about these political issues is to work collaboratively with districts that have been effective at addressing many of the inequities that were listed above. Leaders are encouraged to form relationships with colleagues who share similar challenges and may have already found success with policymakers in identifying, influencing, and responding to equity issues. Ultimately, in order to address the issues of advocating for all students, leaders need

> a more visible way to advocate on behalf of children and families, by writing, e-mailing, or phoning members of local or state legislature, Congress, or Senate. Others may choose to act by getting involved with their local school board, city council, and other committees, such as their local school's parent and teacher association (PTA) or executive boards of agencies that serve children and families. (Royea & Appl, 2009, p. 91)

INFLUENCING POLICIES AND UPHOLDING AND IMPROVING LAWS AND REGULATIONS

Another area in which educators should become more knowledgeable regards how they can uphold and improve educational laws and regulations, as well as how they can personally influence policy development and implementation. Educators should commit themselves to receiving up-to-date information about educational legislation and policy development. A few organizations that keep educators abreast of these issues are the American Association of School Administrators (www.aasa .org), the National Association of Elementary School Principals (www .naesp.org), the National Association of Secondary School Principals (www.principals.org), the National Council of Professors of Educational Administration, the Center on Education Policy (www.cep-dc .org), and the National Education Association (www.nea.org). While leaders are expected to uphold educational laws and regulations, they must also educate teachers, parents, and students about the impact of laws on all of the stakeholders in the school environment. The effective leader attempts to influence legislative developments before they become laws through active participation in state and national organizations and committees.

Educational leaders can no longer sit on the sidelines while policies and legislative mandates are created by politicians and then complain about how detrimental these mandates are at improving student achievement. With the creation and implementation of federal and state mandates such as the No Child Left Behind Act or any other policies that affect learning opportunities, educators must become active participants in these policy processes. It is not enough to walk into our schools and classrooms, close the door, and teach our students. Leaders need to be advocates for the children and ensure that the policies and mandates are built upon the voices of trained educators and not by career politicians who dabble in education.

Eliminating Barriers to Achievement

As educators we need to look beyond barriers to determine the best ways to educate all students. We are aware of many barriers that impede a child's ability to be successful in school, but are any of these appropriate reasons for allowing children to fail. Children come to us from a variety of social, emotional, racial, religious, and socioeconomic backgrounds, and it is our job as educational leaders to provide children with the best teachers and a safe and productive environment. Successful leaders identify strategies to overcome barriers and provide practical instructional models best suited to the needs of all children.

Research has been conducted on many schools that are often described as "90-90-90 schools." These 90-90-90 schools have demographics that equate to 90 percent minority students, 90 percent of the students receive free or reduced lunch, and 90 percent of the students are meeting or exceeding state mandates on standardized achievement tests (Reeves, 2004b). The students in these schools would have historically been considered to have many barriers that stood in the way of their academic success. However, these schools have focused on five areas to achieve student success: academic achievement, clear curriculum choices, frequent assessment of student progress with many opportunities for improvement, a strong emphasis on nonfiction writing, and collaborative scoring of student work—and they have been successful (Reeves, 2004b).

The social-emotional learning standards were developed as a means to address many of the deficits that students have that impact their academic acquisition: "When schools implement high-quality social emotional learning (SEL) programs and approaches effectively, academic achievement of children increases, incidence of problem behaviors decreases, the relationships that surround each child are improved, and the climate of classrooms and schools changes for the better" (Elias & Arnold, 2006, p. 5). Many states have implemented the use of SEL standards and are mandating that school districts utilize the standards to deliver appropriate instruction to all students. It is understood that, until students feel socially and emotionally connected to the school environment, they are less likely to be academically successful. This concept goes back as far as Maslow's hierarchy of needs, which states that people need to have their basic physical and emotional needs addressed before any other learning can take place. It would be worthwhile for you, as a leader, to investigate the benefits of SEL for your school and the status of these standards in your district and state.

Proactive leaders are prepared for cultural changes that may occur within their learning communities. Many districts have developed educational equity committees consisting of community members, as mentioned in chapter 8, as a way to proactively address any potential educational equity issues in schools and districts. Collaborative leadership between the district office and school leaders provides proactive and data-driven decision-making in school planning, programs, and structures. When districts are not proactive in addressing the equity barriers that exist in the educational environment, then the leaders become reactionary and solve problems in crisis mode.

BUILDING ON DIVERSE SOCIAL AND CULTURAL ASSETS

If diversity is an asset, then we should use this asset to assist in growing our student successes exponentially. We continuously talk about how the achievement gap should be eliminated by now, but we have not invested well in building social and cultural assets. By investing in these assets, we will provide opportunities for our students' educational growth portfolios to increase. We liken this to a bank account, where you need to deposit more and invest wisely to see any profit in the end. The more we use our students' own social and cultural assets to create well-rounded learning experiences, the more likely the profit in the end will be student success. We have seen student background as a debit that needs to be overcome instead of utilizing it as an asset that should be invested well to see growth: "Most educators have had minimal experience and training in dealing with the kinds of problems that today's children present. Dealing with students' problems ineffectively or misinterpreting a student's inability to learn is common" (Blankenstein, 2010, p. 117). Consider the banking metaphor and the term "capacity utilization." Capacity utilization measures the extent to which a country's productive capacity is actually being used. Ask yourself this: Are your students' productive capacities being used in your schools? By focusing on the assets that our students bring into our classrooms on a daily basis, teachers should be able to create practical learning experiences that build upon these assets instead of seeing these student differences as debits that need to be overcome.

 ## CARING WITH INTENTIONALITY

Take a moment to read the following dispositions and determine a rating for yourself. We challenge you to not only believe strongly in the following dispositions but also take action in what you believe is important.

Dispositions Exemplified in Standard 6

5	4	3	2	1	0
Highly skilled	Proficient	Average	Limited	Little	No skill

The education leader believes in, values, and is committed to . . .

_____ advocate for children and education
_____ influence policies
_____ uphold and improve laws and regulations
_____ eliminate barriers to achievement
_____ build on diverse social and cultural assets

 ASSESSING WITH INTENTIONALITY

Directions

Rate the following items for each standard, with 5 as the highest level of skill ranging to 0 as no skill. Consider your present position and years of leadership experience as you self-assess your performance below. At the end of each standard, reflect on and identify your strengths and challenges, including a final checkup at the conclusion. Your initial preassessment gives you a baseline on your current leadership performance. Once you have completed the exercises provided in *The Courage to Grow*, return to this self-assessment, and retake it to measure your leadership growth.

5	4	3	2	1	0
Highly skilled	Proficient	Average	Limited	Little	No skill

Standard 6: The Education System

Education leaders ensure the success of all students by influencing interrelated systems of political, social, economic, legal, and cultural contexts affecting education to advocate for their teachers' and students' needs.

Leadership Performance Indicators

Element A: Exerting Professional Influence

A leader . . .

Pre   *Post*

_____ _____ facilitates constructive discussions with the public about federal, state, and local laws, policies, regulations, and statutory requirements affecting continuous improvement of educational programs and outcomes. (6A)

_____ _____ actively develops relationships with a range of stakeholders and policymakers to identify, respond to, and influence issues, trends, and potential changes that affect the context and conduct of education. (6B)

_____ _____ advocates for equity and adequacy in providing for students' and families' educational, physical, emotional, social, cultural, legal, and economic needs, so every student can meet educational expectations and policy goals. (6C)

Element B: Contributing to the Educational Policy Environment

A leader . . .

_____ _____ operates consistently to uphold and influence federal, state, and local laws, policies, regulations, and statutory requirements in support of every student learning. (6D)

_____ _____ collects and accurately communicates data about educational performance in a clear and timely way, relating specifics about the local context to improve policies and inform progressive political debates. (6E)

_____ _____ communicates effectively with key decision-makers in the community and in broader political contexts to improve public understanding of federal, state, and local laws, policies, regulations, and statutory requirements. (6F)

_____ _____ advocates for increased support of excellence and equity in education. (6G)

Element C: Policy Engagement

A leader . . .

___ ___ builds strong relationships with the school board, district and state education leaders, and policy actors to inform and influence policies and policymakers in the service of children and families. (6H)

___ ___ supports public policies that provide for present and future needs of children and families and improve equity and excellence in education. (6I)

___ ___ advocates for public policies that ensure appropriate and equitable human and fiscal resources and improve student learning. (6J)

___ ___ works with community leaders to collect and analyze data on economic, social, and other emerging issues that impact district and school planning, programs, and structures. (6K)

___ ___ Standard 6 Total

Standard 6 Leadership Attributes

Personal Strengths:

_____

_____

_____

Personal Challenges:

_____

_____

_____

GROWING WITH INTENTIONALITY: POLITICS OF LEADERSHIP

In order to strengthen your competencies, based on your particular leadership role, review the following exercises. Using the results of your assessment, choose an exercise or two and then write them into the SMART goal format located at the end of this section.

District- and School-Level Administrators

- Identify your local government representatives, and write a letter to them indicating views on pending legislation. (6B, 6F)
- Join national organizations such as the Association of Supervisors and Curriculum Development, the National Association of Secondary School Principals, the National Association of Elementary School Principals, and the American Association of School Administrators. By becoming a member of these national organizations, you will be able to stay current on upcoming legislation and other changes that are coming in the field of education. (6B, 6I)
- Investigate a successful 90-90-90 school to determine what programs have been effectively implemented that made a huge gain in student success. Share these programs with other leaders in your own district to determine the possibility of replicating this initiative in your district. (6C, 6G, 6J)
- Join your state-level organizations similar to the above to stay up to date on statewide changes in educational legislation. (6B, 6I)

Professors in Educational Administration Programs

- Join some of the organizations listed above to get involved and become aware of the most current events and legislation your administrative candidates will experience. (6B, 6I)
- Invite a local government official to talk to the students in your classes about how they prepare for voting on educational issues. Have them share the funding issues related to educational mandates. (6A, 6F)
- Ask your students to talk with their business and finance, student services, or curriculum and instruction assistant superintendent to find out about alternative funding ideas. Review grant-writing procedures from district grants to grants that schools can apply for at the state and national level. (6B, 6C, 6J)
- Have the students investigate a school or district policy: What is the history of the policy? Who oversees the policy implementation? Compare and contrast it to other district policies. (6A, 6B)

Leadership Candidates and Teacher Leaders

- Join one of the national organizations listed above as a teacher leader to stay current on educational legislation. (6B, 6I)
- Interview your principal or a district-level administrator about how they determine teacher evaluation categorization. Also, ask questions related to teacher and staff dismissal and how the process works in your school and district. (6I, 6J)
- Investigate a successful 90-90-90 school to determine what programs have been effectively implemented that had significant impact on student success. Discuss these findings with the leaders in your own school or district to determine the possibility of replicating this initiative in your district. (6C, 6G, 6J)
- Interview your school-level administrator, and ask how they decide on student discipline practices. Review the district's discipline policies prior to this interview, and find areas that you would like to learn more about. (6A, 6B)

INDIVIDUAL LEADERSHIP ACTION PLAN

In each chapter you are asked to create an individual leadership action plan for yourself based on the knowledge and activities that you have learned about. Review your self-assessment results and the "Growing with Intentionality" section, and determine some goals that you will establish.

As a result of reading this chapter, I will take the following actions:

I will improve _____ [specific and measurable item] by _____ [what strategies will be used to succeed] by _____ [when]. I will assess my growth by _____ [what type of measurement will be used].

I will improve _____ [specific and measurable item] by _____ [what strategies will be used to succeed] by _____ [when]. I will assess my growth by _____ [what type of measurement will be used].

LEADERSHIP TOOLS AND RESOURCES FOR GROWTH

American Association of School Administrators:
www.aasa.org

National Association of Elementary School Principals:
www.naesp.org

National Association of Secondary School Principals:
www.principals.org

Center on Education Policy:
www.cep-dc.org

National Education Association:
www.nea.org

8

TRAINING CAMP

Professional Development
with Intentionality

If your school is stuck using (poor professional develop-
ment), consider focusing on a few things: what to teach,
how to teach it, how to meet the needs of individual stu-
dents, and how to build internal capacity.

—Reeves, 2009, p. 63

 LEARNING WITH INTENTIONALITY

Adult learning has been taking place since time began, yet leaders have
not significantly changed the delivery model for adult learning. The
premise that "if we continue to do the same things, we will always get
the same results" is very prevalent in professional development. It is
time we provide staff development with intentionality. This chapter
is designed to be similar to a training camp. Leaders, just like athletes,
need to receive appropriate training in order to strengthen their skills,
along with the skills of the teachers and staff in their schools and departments. This chapter provides concepts of adult learning principles
and many engaged learning processes (ELPs). These ELPs will assist
you in providing professional development that is intentionally deliv-
ered to meet the needs of your adult learners.

BARRIERS TO PROFESSIONAL DEVELOPMENT AND ADULT LEARNING

Leaders face many barriers for successful professional development. The following are common barriers:

1. "Drive-by" professional development that provides short, unessential, and unsustainable learning experiences. Often, districts begin the year with an inspirational speaker to get the teachers and staff members ready for the year ahead but fail to follow up. Please understand, we are not opposed to inspiration, but we do believe that this inspiration needs to be essential and continuous for the staff. For instance, if you bring in an inspirational speaker to discuss the social-emotional impact on student success, staff development for the year should be provided on social-emotional learning practices.

2. "Sit and get" professional development does not actively engage the adults in the learning experiences. How many times have you experienced staff development anxious for the opportunity to engage in more action-based learning activities? Or have you thought it would be preferable to dialogue with colleagues regarding a topic of shared importance? Leaders need to apply the Golden Rule of "do unto others as you would like done unto you" when it comes to professional development. We provide you with many engaged learning practices within this chapter that you can immediately implement in order to provide meaningful learning opportunities within your educational setting.

3. The objectives are not explicitly stated on how the learning experiences will build on what the participants already know. Professional development participants bring a wealth of knowledge to learning experiences, and often facilitators underestimate participants' valuable knowledge and contributions: "Adults want to be the origin of their own learning and will resist learning activities they believe are an attack on their competence" (Speck, 1996, p. 36). Thus, professional development facilitators need to give participants more autonomy over the what, who, how, why, when, and where of their learning.

4. Time is the enemy. Many districts set aside only a minimal amount of time for staff development. Often, leaders need to address district initiatives that may compete with school goals and learning experiences. How can we better utilize limited time to provide interactive, impactful, and practical learning sessions? An effective leader is conscious of restricted time and uses it wisely to provide staff with continuous, effective engaged learning experiences.

5. With so many learning needs, how do we choose? In the field of education, it is difficult to determine a singular focus for professional development. Leaders must determine professional development based on student and staff needs: "To bring out the best in others, leadership must match the development level of the person being led" (Blanchard, 2010, p. 76). Leaders need to determine professional development based on staff needs and each school situation.

ADULT LEARNING PRINCIPLES

Effective leaders understand and implement best practices in adult learning. To prepare for athletic training camps, coaches need to plan for activities and exercises that will improve their athletes' skills so they are able to optimize performance. Leaders, just like successful coaches, need to plan staff development activities that will maximize the skills of teachers. Andragogy, a theory of adult learning, was highlighted in chapter 3 to assist the reader in understanding professional development for adults.

The adult learning principles in chapter 3 were only a small sample of principles or characteristics of adult learning that have been highlighted in research. Consider which of the suggestions listed in this chapter would be most effective for you. Marsha Speck (1996) notes that the following important points of adult learning theory should be considered when professional development activities are designed for educators:

- Adults will commit to learning when the goals and objectives are considered realistic and important to them.

- Adult learners need to see that the professional development learning and their day-to-day activities are related and relevant.
- Adult learners need direct, concrete experiences in which they apply the learning in real work.
- Adult learning has ego involved. Professional development must be structured to provide support from peers and to reduce the fear of judgment during learning.
- Adults need to receive feedback on how they are doing and the results of their efforts. Opportunities must be built into professional development activities that allow the learner to practice the learning and receive structured, helpful feedback.
- Adults need to participate in small-group activities during the learning to move them beyond understanding to application, analysis, synthesis, and evaluation. Small-group activities provide an opportunity to share, reflect, and generalize their learning experiences.
- Adult learners come to learning with a wide range of previous experiences, knowledge, self-direction, interests, and competencies. This diversity must be accommodated in the professional development planning.
- Transfer of learning for adults is not automatic and must be facilitated. Coaching and other kinds of follow-up support are needed to help adult learners transfer learning into daily practice so that it is sustained. (pp. 36–37)

 GROWING WITH INTENTIONALITY: ENGAGED LEARNING PROCESSES

Professional development is increasingly meaningful when leaders utilize engaging and differentiated learning processes. In order to utilize the features of effective adult learning, it is imperative for leaders to create engaging learning processes to make professional development worthwhile for all involved. This part of the chapter shares a variety of engaged learning processes to assist the leader with creating more impactful staff development. These processes will move the organization from knowing to doing and minimize the gap that exists between the two.

Table 8.1. Learning Topics and Processes

Engaged Learning Processes	Brain-storming	Change Process	Team-building	Communication	Culture	Reflective Practice
World Café Process	X	X		X	X	X
Brain Breaks			X		X	
Icebreakers			X	X	X	
Four-Square Process	X	X	X	X	X	X
Clock Buddies	X	X	X	X	X	X
Carousel Process	X	X	X	X	X	
Storyboard	X	X	X	X	X	X
Jigsawing		X	X	X	X	
Team-building Activities		X	X	X	X	X
Learning Walks/Collegial Conversations	X	X		X	X	X
Movie Clips		X	X	X	X	X
Odd and Even Decision-making Processes	X	X	X	X	X	X
Keep, Drop, or Create	X	X	X	X	X	X
Book Talks		X	X		X	X
Myers-Briggs Process		X	X	X	X	X
Colors Activity		X	X	X	X	X
Learning through Metaphors, Puzzles, and Children's Books		X	X	X	X	
LEGO Process		X	X	X	X	
Coins for Conversations	X	X	X	X	X	X
Fist to Five	X	X	X	X	X	
Bridge Activity	X	X	X	X	X	X
Pick Up Sticks		X	X	X	X	X
Communication Processes		X	X	X	X	X
Enjoyment and Laughter	X	X	X	X	X	X

Engaged learning processes can occur in small groups, large groups, or one-to-one situations. We know that many leaders already have utilized engaged learning, but we also understand that leaders are always looking for new and improved ideas to enhance their professional development repertoire. (See table 8.1 for a crosswalk between learning topics and processes.)

Engaged Learning Process Descriptions

World Café Process

This is an inexpensive and easy way for people to engage in a verbal and written communication activity. Place butcher-block paper and markers on all of the tables in the staff development room. The facilitator begins by asking participants to discuss at their table a question or issue. One person will serve as a recorder. At the end of a period of time, the facilitator will ask the recorder to record a summary of the discussion on the butcher paper, with the names of the participants. The group is then asked to rotate to a different table and discuss the response they find from the previous group. This may be repeated several times. One alternative is for the facilitator to change the question/issue after several rotations. Participants should seek out different tables and groups for each round of discussions. The activity concludes with the facilitator and participants posting the butcher-block paper on the wall. Participants gather around and debrief the diverse comments and perspectives.

Note: If you want to use this as a means to make decisions, you could add a component of "power dotting," which allows participants to choose one to three written statements that mean the most to them. The participants are given one to three colored dots that they place on the butcher paper to demonstrate their preference for a particular concept or statement written. A form of consensus may result as participants view the areas with the greatest number of dots. You can learn more about this process at www.theworldcafe.com.

Brain Breaks

Brain breaks have become a popular form of engagement for students and educators. These are quick, one- to two-minute kinesthetic activities that stimulate the brain through simple movements. One website where you will find some brain breaks is www.energizingbrainbreaks.com. These are great for leaders from all levels as well as for the classroom teachers. Other resources you may find beneficial are *Energizing Brain Breaks* by David Sladkey and *Brain Rules: 12 Principles for Surviving and Thriving at Work, Home, and School* by John Medina.

Icebreakers

Even though some people may cringe at the idea of icebreakers, they are important when beginning any learning session. Icebreakers connect participants so they can socially and emotionally learn together. Facilitators use a brief activity in order to prepare the learners, especially those who may not know each other, for the session that will follow. Icebreakers need to provide connections to learning. These may be necessary when you have participants in the learning sessions who have limited relationships with one another. Icebreakers are also important if you have a very large staff that you are trying to bring together in order to form a richer and more cohesive culture.

Four-Square Process

The four-square activity (engaged learning process [ELP] 8.1) is a process to identify visual outcomes of four distinct areas in a topic of staff development. This activity works best by utilizing poster paper and markers to create a large visual depiction for all to see. The facilitator has each team divide the poster paper by drawing a + to separate the paper into four equal squares. This activity may be used to enhance teaming skills by asking a team to visually provide the following areas: team beliefs, a team name and symbol, team guidelines, and teaming artifacts that showcase their successes. We introduced this process to you in chapter 4 as a means to assess resource allocations.

Clock Buddies

This is a communication technique that you can use during a daylong professional development session or throughout the year. Professors have the students complete the clock buddy form at the beginning of the class and then use it throughout the semester (ELP 8.2). Each participant receives a clock that they put their name on and then find twelve people to sign up for specific times when they may meet during the learning sessions. Each time the leader or professor wants to conduct a paired conversation or activity, they announce a specific time and those two people get together and complete the task that has been assigned.

Carousel Process

Multiple questions or focus areas are written on poster paper around the room. Each team is assigned a poster question or topic, and they are to provide as many responses as possible. Teams will record their responses on each poster using a designated (colored) marker. Each team rotates to the remaining posters with their assigned color marker and attempts to add responses not already identified on the other posters. Each team reports back the responses that they contributed to their original posted question or topic. Discuss the overall results of the activity. This is another ELP in which facilitators can use the power-dotting process mentioned in the World Café Process description.

Storyboard

Storyboarding has been used in many corporate as well as educational organizations to visually depict a process from the initiation to the detailing of an action plan. When districts are creating a strategic plan or schools are developing their school improvement plans, they may consider a storyboard process. A storyboard process includes four stages: brainstorming, prioritizing top ideas, an action plan, and a communication plan. This process brings a diverse group of people with a variety of vantage points together with very tangible results. The facilitator asks guiding questions to elicit input and allow for well-structured brainstorming, decision-making, and actions. "Storyboards are also useful for building group unity and agreement, and teams using them tend to find it easier to make decisions. This is because everyone can get involved, and there's a much greater level of enthusiasm and commitment" (Mind Tools, n.d.). At the end of the storyboard process, a plan is developed that is detailed in regard to human and monetary resources that will be utilized to implement the plan. You will find additional information at www.mindtools.com.

Jigsawing

Jigsawing is an activity where people are assigned a chapter or portion of an article to read and report back to the group. This is a great way for a class or staff to learn about a particular topic without having them read the entire book or article. The facilitator gives directions on what each person or group needs to read and then share with others (e.g., oral presentations, PowerPoint, or an engaging activity related to the material).

Team-building Activities

Team-building activities are very useful when you are working on strengthening relationships in a department, school, and or class. One source that we have used to find many icebreakers and team-building activities is www.teampedia.net. Some team-building activities we have used successfully are as follows:

1. Forced Choice: The objective of this activity is to build an understanding about diversity and equity. ELP 8.3 describes the components of this activity along with the directions for the participants and the facilitator.
2. Creating Flags: This activity allows a group to show learning or demonstrate identity. ELP 8.4 gives a brief description of the directions that you give to a team, committee, department, or classroom. This is an engaging process that allows the participants to get to know each other better and create a visual representation of their team identity.
3. Scavenger Hunt: One sure way a culture can be studied and improved is through the use of a cultural scavenger hunt or a cultural archeological dig (exercises 3.2 and 3.3, detailed in chapter 3). Determine the areas that matter most in your school or district (interventions, differentiation, student engagement, student respect, student achievement, teacher professional development, effective instructional practices, classroom management, parent involvement, etc.). Challenge your district office staff, faculty, or class as teams (grade level or departments) to search out and find evidence that relates to these areas. Provide ample time to seek out and *dig up* these artifacts and bring them back to share with others. Leaders should observe carefully what is collected and

described as valuable. Keep this collection of artifacts or record a list of the items collected and the rationale of their importance. For example, one principal placed the artifacts in a school portfolio that was shared with parents, students, district-level administrators, board members, and faculty members.

4. Number Sequencing Process: Do you remember the original plastic handheld number game where you had eight small tiles that you had to slide to place them in the appropriate numerical order? This team-building activity is very similar, but the numbered tiles are placed on the floor, and eight people randomly placed on the numbers attempt to place themselves into the correct sequence by communicating with one another. You need two identical sets of 8" × 11.5" sheets of paper individually numbered and a number from 1 to 9 on each sheet. Place the numbered sheets of paper on the floor with 1, 2, 3 in the first row, then 4, 5, 6 in the second row, and finally 7, 8, 9 in the last row. Position them close enough so the participants can easily step from one number to the next. Then ask eight people to stand on the numbers, leaving one number open. Once they are situated on a number, randomly hand each person a numbered sheet from 1 to 8, different than the one on which they are standing. The task for the group is to work together to horizontally and vertically move themselves physically to the same corresponding number that they are holding. Share the rules: (1) Participants are only allowed to move one square at a time; (2) they cannot move diagonally or trade numbers; (3) they must remain on a numbered square at all times. At the end of the activity, the person who is holding number 1 should be standing on number 1 and so on, until all are in their correct positions. (You can do this activity with multiple groups using multiple number boards.) Participants not involved in the task are assigned as observers to listen and report back during the debriefing portion of the activity. After they have finished this activity, the facilitator debriefs by asking questions such as these: (1) How was leadership demonstrated during this activity? (2) What person's communication style worked better during this process? (3) What did not work well throughout this process? (4) What behaviors did you observe when your colleagues were sequencing themselves? (5) How does this activity reflect communication on your team? Listening? Problem solving?

Learning Walks/Collegial Conversations

This activity is a great way to get people dialoguing with one another about a specific topic or issue. You may want to incorporate this with a clock buddy conversation (ELP 8.2) and then allow the partners to walk and talk either outside or throughout the building. This process can be used when a group needs movement or a brain break as well as to allow time for colleagues to discuss an important issue. The facilitator assigns the participants a topic or a question and a period of time they are given to discuss it. Each learning pair walks and talks on the issue, and returns to share their ideas with the rest of the group. This popular activity results in engagement, relationship building, and collegial feedback.

Movie Clips

Movie clips support a wide range of professional development topics. Examples include *Apollo 13* to support problem solving, *A Bug's Life* to support change, and *Freedom Writers* to highlight equity. Two websites that provide free access to movie clips are YouTube and www.wingclips.com.

Odd and Even Decision-making Processes

One way to engage the entire staff in a decision about a new initiative is to create two groups, numbering off using odd and even numbers. Each group is assigned to develop rationale and research for the topic or initiative they have been given. The even-numbered groups must determine how the initiative is favorable for the district, and the odd groups need to determine how it is not. The leader may want to intentionally create the groups so they have a good mix of diverse people in each group. Once the groups have researched the issue, each group presents the results, solution, or decision to the whole group. This process provides opportunities for the participants to objectively study an issue and listen as their colleagues share their suggestions and insights. The leader, with the input of participants, then considers the recommendations to make a decision.

Keep, Drop, or Create

Learning by Doing: A Handbook for Professional Learning Communities at Work by Richard DuFour and colleagues (2006) provides this concept. This activity allows educators to talk about curriculum, cultural practices, teaming practices, meeting management, communication models, resource allocations, and so forth. The facilitator puts up three big butcher-block sheets of paper and labels them as "keep," "drop," and "create." The participants write down suggested ideas on sticky notes and place them on the appropriate poster paper. Discussion follows on what is suggested to keep, drop, or create. This is another great visual process that can be utilized to help make decisions.

Book Talks

Book talks are a wonderful way to have a district-level team, class, department, or school grow professionally by participating in an engaging discussion about a particular book. We have done this many times both on a volunteer basis and as an all-school book study where every faculty member participated. Book talks are most effective when you have a weekly or monthly schedule to dialogue about a particular section of the book. Each member of the group is asked to facilitate a session. A jigsaw approach and learning partners could also be used. By splitting up the responsibilities, more people can plan for and actively participate in the learning that will take place. Books to consider are *Learning by Doing* (DuFour, DuFour, Eaker, & Many, 2006), *Schools of Fish: Welcome Back to the Reason You Became an Educator* (Strand, Christensen, & Halper, 2006), *Courageous Conversations About Race* (Singleton & Linton, 2006), and *Strategies That Work: Teaching Comprehension to Enhance Understanding* (Harvey & Goudvis, 2000).

Myers-Briggs Process

A great deal of work has been done on the use of personality types and its impact on culture, collaboration, and community development. The use of personality-type preferences allows leaders to view their staffs through a different lens in order to gain a more comprehensive view of the culture. Most leaders understand they have a faculty with diverse personalities. You can obtain the personality-type inventory from many websites and review print resources such as *Differentiated School Leadership* (Kise & Russell, 2007). One website provides an electronic inventory that we have found helpful: www.humanmetrics.com/cgi-win/JTypes1.htm.

Colors Activity

The colors activity, ELP 8.5, is similar to the Myers-Briggs assessment but may be faster and easier to complete to determine personality as equated to a color and the colors of your organization. This engaged learning process has been modified from *What Color Is Your Parachute?* by Richard Bolles. These activities give your class, department, team, or faculty a better understanding of each other and better ways to work more effectively together.

Learning through Metaphors, Puzzles, and Children's Books

We utilize these resources depending on the topic we are presenting. For example, the concept of constructing a puzzle is used to illustrate vision. We will give various pieces of the puzzle to many participants and ask them to come forward to put the puzzle together. We give them no additional information, and ultimately someone may pick up the puzzle box to see what the finished puzzle looks like. We emphasize for the group when they are finished that this is what visions are like: we are all working hard, but if no one knows what the ideal vision is, then we are all contributing random pieces to the "puzzle" or our organizational purpose. We have also used *The Velveteen Rabbit* to illustrate changes that take place in leadership (ELP 8.6). It can be used as great reflective activity for future leadership candidates as well as practicing leaders. Metaphors such as travel provide ideal ways to offer a day of professional development with a travel brochure, destinations, and items to pack for the journey.

LEGO Process

One way we have used props to depict a learning process is to use large LEGO blocks to build the school's vision, mission, and goals. The participants write the mission, vision, and beliefs on different LEGO blocks. They then attach these LEGOs to a base that will become the foundation for the rest of the sculpture. Each team or department then writes SMART goals, which assist in achieving the vision, on different LEGO blocks and adds them to the sculpture. This visual representation could be placed in a trophy case or central location as a focus for the year. You may continue to bring this LEGO creation out during staff meetings and professional development days throughout the year.

Coins for Conversations

Have you ever tried to get more people to participate in staff development discussions? Have you ever tried to get some people to participate less during staff development discussions? "Coins for Conversations" is a way to get everyone to actively engage in a learning conversation in an equitable manner. The facilitator will give everyone in the group five play coins. Each time a person has something to share in the discussion, they will take one of their coins and place it in the middle of the table. This is a visual process that highlights how engaged participants are in a discussion. For the participants who only used one or two coins, the leader may invite the person to respond more in the future. If participants used up their coins quickly, you may need to encourage this person to reduce their interactions with the group. This activity is a visual reminder of the need to share talk time and ideas in group discussions.

Fist to Five

This is a very quick consensus process to determine how a group feels about a particular topic. Once the leader or professor has shared a concept with the participants, he or she asks the group to share how comfortable or confident they are about the topic by putting up either a fist if they feel very uncomfortable or one to five fingers, with five representing a very high level of comfort. This gives the entire group a range of understanding or comfort about a topic in a quick and easy manner.

Bridge Activity

Complete the bridge activity as a means to understand present culture and how we need to bridge between current and future cultural issues (exercise 3.4). Sample directions: Teams or departments identify their present cultural best practices in the left column of the bridge. Then they need to discuss and write their dream best practices in the area of cultural enhancements inside the right column. Once the participants have identified their present and future best cultural practices, they need to brainstorm potential strategies to make their ideal culture a reality and list them in the middle column. This activity can also be applied to many other issues that arise in schools (e.g., grading practices, resource allocations, space usage).

Pick Up Sticks

Organizational change may be related to playing the childhood game of Pick Up Sticks. You can find adult-sized Pick Up Sticks on the Internet at Trainers Warehouse. Executing organizational change is like playing Pick Up Sticks because you want to carefully make moves while not disturbing others. These sticks represent the difficulty of isolating one decision from another. Surprises pop up everywhere. Here are some lessons for change from the game of Pick Up Sticks.

- Isolate change: Address first those issues that stand alone. Dealing with interlocking problems is more difficult and requires greater care.
- Focus: Work on only one issue (stick) at a time.
- Be slow and deliberate: Change, like Pick Up Sticks, requires patience and concentration. Move slowly and plan carefully.
- Watch for interlocks: Sometimes sticks rest on each other in an interlocked loop: A on B, B on C, and C on A. Removing one disturbs the others. Be aware of issues that interrelate. When you have no choice but to act, do the best you can.

Communication Processes

Another activity that works on effective communication and team building involves one participant who is blindfolded and another participant who is verbally guiding them through some type of obstacle or activity. Of course, we need to ensure that it is a safe environment for all, but it does highlight various communication styles that your class, department, or faculty use to communicate with one another. The facilitator sets up a few low obstacles that the blindfolded person needs to maneuver around using the verbal directions of their partner.

Note: A variation of this activity is to have two partners sit back to back; one partner describes a picture of geometric shapes to the person behind, who draws the same geometric shapes appropriately on a blank sheet of paper. You can either create overlaying geometric shapes or find an activity similar to this on any team-building website. Once the activity is completed, the facilitator asks debriefing questions such as follows: (1) Describe the communication efforts that were most successful and least successful, and why. (2) How does this activity represent issues in communication and teaming? (3) What can you apply from this activity to one of your teams? Observers also play a part by watching and sharing the communication strategies that are attempted.

Enjoyment and Laughter

Finally, even though all of these engaged learning processes are utilized to enhance professional development, it is imperative that they also be enjoyable to the participants and even elicit some laughter. Since one of the adult learning principles states that learning is directly proportional to the amount of enjoyment adults have in a given learning environment, facilitators need to foster enjoyment as an outcome of learning.

Delivery of Engaged Learning Processes

The delivery of the ELPs that have been shared in this chapter can be conducted in a variety of ways. Sometimes we have very knowledgeable in-district trainers in our own backyard: teachers, professors, social workers, community members, or principals. Leaders and professors can also use teams of teachers to deliver professional development. Consider using the term "faculty learning sessions" in place of the traditional faculty meeting to enrich the learning experiences of teachers and administrators. During the faculty learning sessions, invite teams of teachers to deliver a lesson on topics, such as best instructional practices in various disciplines, classroom management strategies, diversity and equity issues, and enhancing parent involvement.

Another delivery process that has been successful is to change the location of staff development. For instance, if you always have staff meetings or department meetings in one space, consider having your meetings in different spaces throughout the year. We know this depends on the size of the faculty or department, but if it is small enough, it is nice to have the meetings in different teachers' classrooms so they can host the meeting. This allows teachers to see different classrooms and to learn how others organize their spaces.

Facilitators can also use various techniques to change where people sit during staff or department meetings. Changing seating practices during a meeting may allow more cross-grade-level or cross-department conversations that are often limited in school settings.

CARING WITH INTENTIONALITY

As future and current leaders and professors, we have a desire to provide strong and effective learning experiences for the adults in our organizations. We understand that, if we can find effective methods to strengthen the skills of teachers, then ultimately that knowledge and understanding will be beneficial to overall student success. We hope that by providing you with many engaged learning processes we have assisted you with preparing and delivering enriched professional development that will impact students for years to come.

Engaged Learning Process 8.1: Four-Square Activity

DEFINING AND ESTABLISHING TEAM PURPOSE AND IDENTITY: EDUCATIONAL LEADERSHIP CLASS

Team Name and Motto	*Roles*
"The Mixers"	We are all the bakers
"Come for the pie; stay for the education"	~ Recorder:
	~ Liaison:
	~ Technology Rep:
	~ Materials:
	~ Facilitator:
Team Beliefs	*Mixer Guiding Principles*
~ Children are our future	"Our recipe for success"
~ Every ingredient is vital for success	~ Wash your hands and begin with open minds
~ Leadership guides the process	~ Add equal parts of contribution and responsibility to team
~ We believe that ideas will be sprinkled in a safe environment	~ Mix in mutual support and respect
	~ Mix all with joint decision-making

Engaged Learning Process 8.2: Clock Buddy Sign-up

My Name: _____

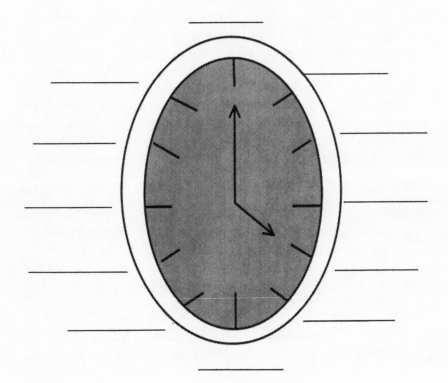

Engaged Learning Process 8.3: Forced Choice Activity
(www.teampedia.net/wiki/index.php?title=Forced_Choice)

Appropriate group size: medium or large

Supplies: The following identity signs should be printed, and masking tape could be used: race, gender, socioeconomic class, sexual orientation, immigration status, ability/disability status, religion, and age.

Set-up: Place the eight signs on the walls around a large room so they can be read by the participants as they move around. Ask the participants to come to the middle of the room for instructions. Explain to the group that there are two parts to the activity. One is a silent and reflective part when they are together at the beginning of the room, and one is sharing with a group once everyone has made a choice for a particular statement.

Directions: The facilitator explains that he/she will read a statement and the participants are to choose one of the eight parts of their identity to complete the statement. Each person is encouraged to choose for themselves through reflection where they go in the room. This is the silent part of the activity. Once everyone has made a choice, ask them to share in their group why they selected that part of their identity to complete the statement. The facilitator should allow for several minutes of discussion and then have the participants return silently to the middle where they will hear another statement to complete. The facilitator repeats the same process after each statement.

Statements

1. The part of my identity that I am most aware of on a daily basis is _____.
2. The part of my identity that I am the least aware of on a daily basis is _____.
3. The part of my identity that was most emphasized in my family growing up was _____.
4. The part of my identity that serves as my primary compass for my work style is _____.
5. The part of my identity that garners me the most privilege is _____.

6. The part of my identity that I believe is the most misunderstood by others is _____.
7. The part of my identity that I feel is difficult to discuss with others who identify differently is _____.

Reflective Questions

1. How did you feel about completing this activity? Often, participants realize how much they have in common with their colleagues and this creates more team building.

_____

_____

_____

2. Did you feel uncomfortable or find it difficult to finish any particular statements?

_____

_____

_____

3. Why is this activity important for team and relationship building?

_____

_____

_____

Engaged Learning Process 8.4: Team Flag Creations

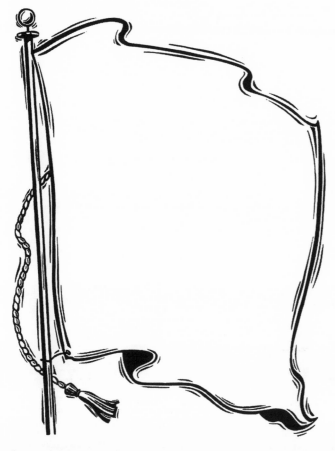

In your groups, you need to design a unique flag that symbolizes your individualities as well as your similarities. You will have approximately thirty minutes to create your flags, and then we will have a flag presentation back as a whole group. You can use whatever you have at your disposal in the building to create your unique designs, but keep in mind everyone should be able to see each other's unique qualities as well as your overarching similarities. Be creative and allow each member of the group to participate in their own way. We will "fly" these flags in the building, so keep that in mind as you create your size.

Engaged Learning Process 8.5: True Colors

This activity is designed to identify your personality style. We will examine the characteristics associated with each style when you are finished completing the activity.

In table 8.2 are groups of word clusters printed horizontally in rows. Score each group of words, giving yourself 4 for the most like you, 3 for the second, 2 for third, and finally 1 for the least like you. Each row will have one of each number. Don't spend a lot of time thinking about it—simply go with what comes to mind first.

Table 8.2.   True Colors—Word Clusters

SET 1	Active Opportunistic Spontaneous A___	Parental Traditional Responsible B___	Authentic Harmonious Compassionate C___	Versatile Inventive Competent D___
SET 2	Curious Conceptual Knowledgeable E___	Unique Empathetic Communicative F___	Practical Sensible Dependable G___	Competitive Impetuous Impactful H___
SET 3	Loyal Conservative Organized I___	Devoted Warm Poetic J___	Realistic Open-Minded Adventurous K___	Theoretical Seeking Ingenious L___
SET 4	Concerned Procedural Cooperative M___	Daring Impulsive Fun N___	Tender Inspirational Dramatic O___	Determined Complex Composed P___
SET 5	Philosophical Principled Rational Q___	Vivacious Affectionate Sympathetic R___	Exciting Courageous Skillful S___	Orderly Conventional Caring T___

Input your results into table 8.3, which shows the resulting colors of various personality styles.

Table 8.3. True Colors—Key

A	B	C	D
H	G	F	E
K	I	J	L
N	M	O	P
S	T	R	Q
Total:	Total:	Total:	Total:
Orange	*Gold*	*Blue*	*Green*

You have differing levels of each color in your personality. However, the highest number most describes your personality.

_____

_____

_____

What color personality are you? (See table 8.4 for descriptions of each style.)

_____

Table 8.4. True Colors—Personality Descriptions

Orange (Accommodating)	Blue (Diverging)
At home and work I: ★ Become bored and restless with routine and structure ★ Prefer independence and freedom ★ Enjoy my physical abilities and enjoy using tools and objects ★ Am a natural performer ★ Prefer activities where there are shared activities and interests ★ Like to explore new ways to energize my relationships within my family	At home and work I: ★ Try to influence others so they can lead more significant lives ★ Like to pursue interests and abilities in the arts communication and education ★ Like to help others ★ Am adept at motivating and interacting with others ★ Look for and work toward harmonious relationships
As a child I: ★ Had difficulties fitting into academic routines ★ Learned more by doing and experiencing than reading and listening ★ Needed physical involvement in the learning process ★ Was motivated by competition and fun	As a child I: ★ Was extremely imaginative and found it difficult to fit into the structure of school ★ Reacted strongly to rejection and any kind of discord ★ Sought recognition and responded to encouragement rather than competition

Green (Converging)	Gold (Assimilating)
At home and work I: ★ Am conceptual and an independent thinker ★ Believe work is play ★ Like to explore ideas and deal with innovation ★ Prefer to move on once I have perfected an idea ★ Let my head rule my heart ★ Dislike repetition, so it is difficult for me to continuously express feelings that I believe are obvious	At home and work I: ★ Provide stability and can maintain organization handle details and hard work ★ Believe that work comes before play ★ Am serious and tend to have traditional, conservative views about family, love, and marriage ★ Demonstrate love and affection through practical things that I do for others
As a child I: ★ Appeared to be older than my years ★ Focused on my greatest interests and achieved in subjects I found stimulating ★ Was impatient with drill and routine ★ Questioned authority and found it necessary to respect teachers before I could learn	As a child I: ★ Followed rules and regulations ★ Understood and respected authority ★ Did well with school routine

Engaged Learning Process 8.6:
Lessons from the Velveteen Rabbit

What does it mean to be real?

> For the Velveteen Rabbit, becoming real meant learning to be truly himself and not a version of something he thought he was supposed to be. Because it's based on our individuality, real is different for everyone, just as life's meaning is different for everyone, too. But we can agree that in all cases it includes feelings of happiness and contentment, work that is engaging, relationships that feel satisfying, and enough love that we don't feel alone in the world. The Velveteen Principles can help you discover and develop your real self, live with empathy and establish satisfying relationships. And the qualities that make us real, including courage, honesty, gratitude, flexibility and honesty, help us to connect with others and live in a more engaged, appreciative and deeply satisfying way. Once you are real, and you know that everything you say and do matters to others, you can also understand that we each leave a mark on the world that remains long after we're gone. (excerpts taken from author Margery Williams)

The Velveteen Principles: Reflective Practice

Consider an example in your own life, teaching, or leadership where you have demonstrated the Velveteen Principles:

#1: Real is possible: _____

#2: Real is a process: _____

#3: Real is emotional: _____

#4: Real is empathetic: _____

#5: Real is courageous: _____

#6: Real is honest: _____

#7: Real is generous: _____

#8: Real is grateful: _____

#9: Real can be painful: _____

#10: Real is flexible: _____

#11: Real love endures: _____

#12: Real is ethical: _____

Which of the twelve principles have you most demonstrated?

Identify one principle in which you wish to improve. Set a goal for ways you can improve, and apply these principles to your teaching and leadership.

PROFESSIONAL DEVELOPMENT DAY

March to Your Own Beat

Institute Day Agenda

*You can come up with unique names for each of the groups to work with your theme for the day. This particular theme was music, so each group had a different type of music as their team name.

Table 8.5. Professional Development Day Format

Time	Differentiation	Team Building	Silly Sports	Core Standards	Probes
9:20–9:50	Country	Break	R & B	Alternative	Rock
9:52–10:12	Rock	Country	Break	R & B	Alternative
10:14–10:44	Alternative	Rock	Country	Break	R & B
10:46–11:16	R & B	Alternative	Rock	Country	Break
11:18–11:48	Break	R & B	Alternative	Rock	Country

1. 7:30–8:00: Breakfast in Media Center
2. 8:00–8:15: Discuss the Day
3. 8:15–9:15: Differentiated Math Presentation: K.D. and V.W. (Media Center)
4. Break-out Sessions

Groups

Differentiation—Computer Lab (differentiation specialist and special ed. teacher)

Silly Sports and Goofy Games—Gymnasium (two classroom teachers with administration degrees)

Probes—Room 402 (two classroom teachers from different grades, one with an administration degree)

Core Standards—Room 301 (assistant principal)

Team Building—Room 201 (classroom teacher with administration degree and principal)

Break-out Groups

Create the groups by mixing teams and departments to allow for more relationship building as well as more focused learning since colleagues are working with different groups of people. Have the groups switch every thirty to forty-five minutes based on the length of the staff development day. Make sure every person attends each group. You could even design it to allow for the participants to have one session open so they can observe at least one other break-out session. You can play music over the public address system when the session is ended and then stop the music when they arrive at their next room.

1. 11:50: Media Center: Reflections and Feedback on the morning
2. 12:00–1:30: Work with grade-level teams to plan based on the information gleaned from the breakout sessions
3. 1:30: Have a restful afternoon!

This agenda may change due to more pressing issues needing to be addressed.

LEADERSHIP TOOLS AND RESOURCES FOR GROWTH

Information about adult learning principles:
www.andragogy.net

Brain breaks:
www.energizingbrainbreaks.com

Team-building activities:
www.mindtools.com
www.teampedia.net

Processing ideas and strategies:
www.theworldcafe.com

Inspirational video clips:
www.wingclips.com

Online personality assessment:
www.humanmetrics.com

9

CELEBRATING WITH INTENTIONALITY

Carpe diem: Seize and celebrate the day.

LEARNING WITH INTENTIONALITY

Why Celebrations?

Celebration. Recognition. Gratitude. Encouragement. What do each of these terms have in common? When implemented with intentionality by leaders, educators, or professors, there can be tremendous benefits for all the stakeholders. Why has celebration become a topic of focus in education in recent years? The research in organizational culture and professional learning communities increasingly points to the importance of meeting the emotional, social, and professional needs of its members, and this can frequently be accomplished through recognizing and celebrating success (Kouzes & Posner, 2003; DuFour, DuFour, Eaker, & Many, 2006). Unfortunately, some educators fall into the mind-set that individual recognition suggests preferential treatment, causing some individuals to feel excluded or creating a division among teachers. Another common notion regarding celebrations is that it is an elite and subjective process. However, educational experts such as Richard DuFour (2006) provide four guidelines for broad, inclusive, and genuine organizational celebration: (1) explicitly state the purpose of the celebration; (2) make celebration everyone's responsibility, not just the school leaders'; (3) establish a clear link between the recognition and the behavior or commitment you are attempting to encourage or reinforce; and (4) create opportunities for many recipients to be recognized, appreciated, and celebrated.

Celebrations are at the core of our human existence. One organization that strives to continuously demonstrate a spirit of appreciation and celebration is Southwest Airlines. If you have flown with this airline, you already know that they value happiness, humor, and recognition.

> Without celebration, we are robbed of our life and vitality that energizes the human spirit. Latent and underdeveloped though it might be, there is within our nature as human beings an inherent need to sing, dance, love, laugh, mourn, tell stories, and celebrate. . . . There is no culture in the world that doesn't embrace some form of festivity. To deny our need to celebrate is to deny a part of what it means to be human. . . . When we work in an environment where we are not encouraged to express this festive nature, our celebrative faculties, like unused muscles, begin to atrophy. (Freiburg & Freiburg, 1998, p. 177)

A leader has tremendous influence over the cultural happiness that exists in a school environment. What is it about some leaders that cause them to naturally seek and recognize cultural happiness? Elle Allison has studied leaders who choose happiness for themselves and, as a result, demonstrate a greater degree of meaningful work and make more of a difference in their organizations (Reeves & Allison, 2009). Reeves and Allison provide a model to help leaders gain awareness of choices that can increase happiness and conduct meaningful work; this model includes an assessment of these choices and is available at www.renewalcoaching.com. The assessment is a means to create a profile based on a leader's choices, engagement, and performance. Ultimately, the research of Doug Reeves and Elle Allison reminds leaders that emotions such as happiness are a vital contributor to both individual and organizational satisfaction. The use of organizational celebrations enhances the intention of a leader to recognize meaningful work and accomplishments.

What are the areas considered for celebrations in your organization? This chapter provides three areas as criteria for celebrating success: individual performance, achievement of formal and informal goals, and professional growth. Recommended resources such as *Encouraging the Heart* (Kouzes & Posner, 2003) provide a rationale for why encouragement is essential to the success of an organization. The following is a tribute to James Kouzes and Barry Posner's efforts to help leaders to intentionally embrace emotions such as passion and encouragement as vital competencies for success:

> Leadership authorities James M. Kouzes and Barry Z. Posner say employees perform best when their contributions are genuinely appreciated. Unfortunately, the two contend, most executives have not mastered the decidedly soft-management skill of "encouragement" that fosters such behavior. In *Encouraging the Heart*, they examine how this type of compassionate supervision is becoming a critical part of successful management today, and through example and suggestion they describe how readers can establish the process in their own businesses.
>
> This is not a book about glad-handing and backslapping, gold stars, and payoffs. It's about the importance of linking rewards and appreciation to standards of excellence. It's about why encouragement is absolutely essential to sustaining people's commitment to organizations and outcomes. It's about the hard work it takes to get extraordinary things done in organizations, and it's about ways to enhance your own ability in—and comfort with—recognizing and celebrating the achievements of others. (Amazon.com review)

The responsibility to celebrate success is not limited to the formal leaders of an organization. The book *Fish! Tales* (Lundin, Christensen, Paul, & Strand, 2002), for example, emphasizes a shared cultural responsibility by all stakeholders to recognize the achievement and contributions of each member of an organization or a community. If you believe celebration is important for educators but fear you lack the *creativity* to develop celebration activities for people in your organization, this chapter will provide you with practical ideas.

RECOGNIZING INDIVIDUAL HIGH STANDARDS

Individual recognition of high performance is one criterion for recognition. High performers are often the next inspiring leaders and serve as models and mentors for many others. When leaders intentionally recognize the hard work of others, they validate the values and standards of the organizational culture. Leaders who show appreciation and gratitude for the performance of others increase the likelihood of a positive work environment and greater work satisfaction of the members of the organization. Sonia Lyubomirsky, a professor of psychology, has studied happiness and finds gratitude to be an important contributor: "People who are consistently grateful have been found to be relatively happier, more energetic, and more hopeful and to report experiencing more frequent positive emotions" (Lyubomirsky, 2007, 90). Although everyone appreciates financial rewards, public acknowledgment and appreciation for a job well done is also a great motivator. Individual accomplishments foster positive relationships among those who recognize the achievements and those who are demonstrating the highest of standards.

Educators may have to look to their counterparts in business to improve in recognizing personal and organization success. Longtime companies such as Successories (www.successories.com), Master Teacher (www.masterteacher.com), or Baudville (www.baudville.com) provide hundreds of categories, themes, and gifts to recognize and honor high performance. These organizations have celebration products that highlight the following accomplishments: high performance in achievement, attitude, believing and succeeding, excellence, innovation, leadership, service, and teamwork. Leaders should collaboratively develop a plan to support and recognize these accomplishments.

Recognition efforts reinforce the individual performer and remind members of the high standards desired for all. Often schools avoid the *business approach* to recognizing others, such as the "employee of the month," for fear it will cause resentment or disharmony by those not recognized. This is not the case when leaders make individual recognition frequent and relevant to everyone. Shared methods of recognition by those other than the leader support the cultural value for recognition and reduce the likelihood that some members will feel overlooked when recognition occurs.

ACHIEVEMENT OF FORMAL AND INFORMAL GOALS

A second criterion for celebration is the successful achievement of formal and informal organizational goals. These may be goals set by the entire school, a team, or a department. In order for leaders to utilize goals as a measure of success, it is important to consider setting goals that are measurable. The use of SMART goals referenced in the previous chapters has become a means for goal setting to be standardized in a way that goals can be measured. When goals are specific, measurable, and time established, there is a greater likelihood that they will be attained and successful results celebrated.

One of the top recognitions that a school community can experience is the National Blue Ribbon Award for Excellence. The Blue Ribbon Schools Program has existed since 1982 through the U.S. Department of Education. It honors public and private elementary, middle, and high schools that demonstrate exemplary performance or have significantly improved student achievement, especially among disadvantaged students. The program spotlights schools each year that demonstrate high performance in teaching and leadership that results in high student achievement. Four criteria are used for selection as a National Blue Ribbon School: school culture, high expectations, educating the whole child, and leadership. While this recognition may be considered out of reach for some reading this manual, you can look back at the schools formerly honored and ask yourself, "What are they doing that we are not?" The answer may surprise you and may also convince you to take steps to challenge your school to earn this top U.S. national award. Effective leaders provide the best opportunities for students and do not settle for less. The National Blue Ribbon process and outcome may have a powerful impact on your school. The question leaders must ask is this: Why not seek out the best opportunities for students, teachers, and the school community?

When goals are clearly developed, leaders are in a position to recognize individual, team, or organizational achievements. The school improvement plan has been a central focus for many schools and should be a critical focus to recognize success. Although many schools have high-performing teams, without setting and measuring goals, teams are rarely recognized for their success. A superintendent and personnel in the district office could also celebrate the success of a school that has met its school improvement goals, yearly progress, or state test results. Ideas to celebrate teams, departments, and schools are provided at the end of this chapter.

CELEBRATING PROFESSIONAL GROWTH

A third criterion for celebration is professional growth. Efforts for individuals to develop new skills and grow in professional competencies are not easily accomplished and should be measured and celebrated among the top organizational values. The growth and development of teams should also be noted as an ideal area of celebration, although this is more likely when teams utilize a common teaming assessment.

One area that is often overlooked in celebrations and achievements is professional performance. Most teacher leaders, administrators, and professors experience an annual performance evaluation to compare and celebrate improved performance from one year to the next. This chapter provides a self-assessment, from *Encouraging the Heart* by Kouzes and Posner (2003), for leaders to measure competencies in recognizing individual and organizational success.

CELEBRATING *THE COURAGE TO GROW* ASSESSMENT RESULTS

Chapter 9 is an opportunity for each reader to review and celebrate his or her growth throughout this *Courage to Grow* manual. Readers should reflect on the assessments and goals they have established for themselves in each chapter and note areas of growth. Once you have completed the activities and exercises from each chapter, you should be prepared to return and complete the standards' postassessments that are provided in chapters 2–7. Determine the standards where you made the greatest growth and the areas where you would like to improve. In what areas can you celebrate significant growth? What areas need further development? What questions and issues are still lingering that you will want to address regarding your own growth and development as a leader? In what areas will you celebrate success?

 ### CARING WITH INTENTIONALITY

Personalizing Celebration to Your Culture

Guidelines can be helpful for leaders to celebrate success and recognize high standards. The seven guidelines from *Encouraging the Heart* (Kouzes & Posner, 2003) provide a framework for leaders and educators to recognize positive behavior within the organization. These essentials include the following: (1) set clear expectations; (2) expect the best; (3) pay attention; (4) personalize recognition; (5) celebrate data and results; (6) tell the story; and (7) celebrate together. These are simple essential reminders that provide guidelines for how celebrations can be incorporated to ensure academic, professional, and personal benefits.

Putting Celebration into Practice

The following celebration practices will assist the leader with ideas to recognize individual, team, and organizational achievements. Feel free to mix and match any of the ideas described to create and personalize celebrations in your organization.

Children's Stories

Children's stories can be a positive way to highlight achievements and positive accomplishments. Examples of favorites include Dr. Seuss's *Oh, the Places You'll Go!*, *The Little Engine that Could*, *The Velveteen Rabbit*, *Stone Soup*, and *The Giving Tree*. Each includes a positive message and provides a gift within the book itself.

Collective Contributions to Recognition

Invite your organizational members to play an active part in recognizing individual accomplishments. Provide a variety of categories, and ask members to nominate their peers for each. These might be compared to the Academy Awards for movies or the People's Choice Awards for television. Examples might include the Strong Support Award, Outstanding Team Member, the Collaboration and Caring Award, High-Energy Prize, the Balance of Work and Fun Award, and the Difference-Maker Award. Provide a certificate of achievement or trophy for each of these honors. Remember to provide many voices in who is recognized as well as many winners.

Educational Awards and Symbols

The field of education provides many symbols that can be presented as certificates or items that represent accomplishments. The traditional symbols include apples, chalkboards, books, and countless others that can be searched for in any clip art collection and personalized for individual recognition.

Heroes and High Performers

High performers might be compared to heroes. High performers demonstrate courage, action, and the conviction to be successful. These characteristics are also found in our childhood superheroes such as Batman, Wonder Woman, and Spiderman. Today's heroes might also serve as a framework to recognize high performers. Leaders should consider examples of today's high performers as a means to recognize the high achievers within your own organization.

Incremental Encouragement

Encouragement should not be delayed until the conclusion of a large project or process. Often the encouragement is most valued as participants accomplish significant hurdles or small steps. A good comparison is the process of weight loss. Celebration is needed throughout the tough process of losing weight, not only at the end with final results. Identify the benchmarks of accomplishments for projects in your school or organization, and intentionally recognize the successful increments of progress. Incremental recognition may be verbal praise, a symbolic token of appreciation, or a thank-you note.

Metaphors

A metaphor, a figure of speech in which an implied comparison is made between two unlike things that have something in common, can provide a creative image for recognizing accomplishments. Common examples include growth compared to a garden, leadership compared to a compass, and building compared to an architect.

Movies

Past and present movies can serve as themes for celebration. Less serious movies such as *Happy Feet* (diversity), *A Bug's Life* (change and leadership), and *Finding Nemo* (growth) can be a playful and effective way to recognize a wide variety of topics and individuals. Single or multiple movie clips can serve to celebrate success. Be sure to remember the hot, buttered popcorn.

Music

Music is a significant part of practically all cultural events. Music can serve as a backdrop for a celebration or as a gift to recognize others. The personalized gift of a CD of favorite music can be created and given as a thank you to recognize success. Songs such as "Celebration" (by Cool and the Gang) and "Simply the Best" (by Tina Turner) may be a musical tribute to individuals, teams, or a faculty.

Praise—Public or Private

There is no doubt that praise can be a very simple yet powerful motivator. Leaders must be sensitive to using the appropriate venue, private or public, when using praise for individual or group recognition. Different approaches may depend on the individual personality or the reason for the praise. Public praise is a good reminder of the organizational values. Private praise is best suited for deepening a relationship that lets someone know that they are appreciated and noticed.

Recognition and Celebration Partners

This activity involves asking each member to randomly select the name of a colleague, and then to support and encourage that colleague. Often this is done at Christmastime as "Secret Santa," where over a period of time someone secretly provides another person with favors, favorite items, and special recognition. Why limit this support to Christmastime? This can serve to build relationships at the start of the year and provide support late in the year when morale may lessen. Determine a final date for the recognition partners, and provide a social time where all the participants identify their partner.

Note: This is a great activity with leadership candidates in a graduate course for principal preparation.

Stories that Inspire

There are many sources for stories that inspire. Go to Simple Truths, an excellent website (www.simpletruths.com) for obtaining hundreds of books and stories for motivational and inspirational gifts. Simple Truths is a motivating resource that offers gifts and inspirational stories for every occasion and celebration. This website also provides videos a leader may want to utilize to inspire educators or recognize colleagues that inspire others.

Sweet Tooth

For the most part, we all enjoy sweet treats. Participants in this activity begin with a large cookie that represents their day. Candy toppings are provided and added to the cookie to reflect each person's feelings and behavior for that day. Favorite toppings are labeled and might including the following: Red Hots—frustration; gummi candies—being stretched thin; Three Musketeers—collaborated with others; Good & Plenty—helped many others; Snickers—laughed often; whipped cream— let out some bottled-up feelings; and caramel—managed to get through a sticky situation. Think of some of your own favorite toppings to add. Pair up with a partner and share your day.

Symbols

The use of symbols is a common way for organizations to visually identify their culture, values, and high performers. The most traditional symbol is a mascot. For many organizations, it may be symbols that represent a hero, famous person, object, or items that the organization has created to recognize past or present success. An object may be developed as a traveling trophy earned and passed among members of a faculty, graduate class, or district office as a valued icon within the culture.

Themes

Themes provide a common focus for a group and can be found through movies, social issues, books, music, and sports. A theme such as baseball, for example, would reflect baseball terms (innings), rules (foul ball), scoring (home run), mishaps (outs), foods (hot dogs), awards (all star), and roles (manager), to name a few. Favorite resources such as *Fish! Tales* (Lundin, Christensen, Paul, & Strand, 2002) encourage a fish theme or the *Wizard of Oz* for teamwork. A theme of "Navigating to New Heights"

CELEBRATING WITH INTENTIONALITY

may allow for travel symbols and language. Brainstorm ideas and ways to develop a theme for your school, department, or team. Use your theme at quarterly celebrations of individual, team, or professional growth.

Traveling Trophies

A favorite symbol can also serve as a traveling trophy to celebrate success. In one school, the principal individually recognized faculty members with a golden apple for student advocacy. The principal asked each recipient to pass the golden apple on to someone else they recognized and respected as a student advocate. Over time, each of the golden apples discreetly traveled throughout the faculty, recognizing countless peers for their dedication to students. A second example was a middle school that used several large, high-top tennis shoes (size 22) and filled each with chocolate treats. These were passed among teachers as recognition for going the extra mile for students. Each Monday, the tennis shoe was passed on as recognition to another teacher.

Certificates of Accomplishment

Certificates provide a written document of a form of accomplishment. *The Courage to Grow* has been an accomplishment for each reader and, therefore, it seems only fitting that the final chapter of this leadership growth manual provides you, the reader, with a certificate of leadership growth and development (found at the end of this chapter).

A leader's qualities and characteristics have a tremendous influence on school culture. Kouzes and Posner (2002) developed a survey (the Leadership Practices Inventory) that asked people which, among a list of common characteristics of leaders, were, in their experiences of being led by others, the top leadership qualities they look for, admire, and would *willingly* follow. For over twenty years, they managed to compile results from seventy-five thousand people. Take a moment to number the leadership characteristics that you value most in leaders. If you would like to find out as a leader what your staff feels are your most important characteristics, you can copy the list and have each person identify your top qualities. A professor may want to use this to generate self-awareness from leadership candidates, or a superintendent could use it with the administrative team. Discuss the results of this exercise to appreciate how similar or different a leader and staff may be regarding desirable leadership qualities.

Directions: Place the numbers 1–10 next to the qualities you most admire in a leader, with 1 being your top choice.

_____ Honesty
_____ Forward looking
_____ Competent
_____ Inspiring
_____ Intelligent
_____ Fair minded
_____ Broad minded
_____ Supportive
_____ Straightforward
_____ Dependable
_____ Cooperative
_____ Determined
_____ Imaginative
_____ Ambitious
_____ Courageous
_____ Caring
_____ Mature
_____ Loyal
_____ Self-controlled
_____ Independent

 GROWING WITH INTENTIONALITY: CELEBRATING

Leadership Growth and Reflection: Developing a Personal Leadership Fitness Plan

This chapter has focused on celebrations. The decisive celebration is the culmination of each reader's knowledge, goals, and growth. Go back into the manual, and complete the postassessment for each standard (chapters 2–7). Place three to five of your primary goals in the performance plan below. Reflect on your goals and self-assessment scores. In which areas did you experience the most significant growth? What does this suggest for your competencies as a leader? Just like any great athlete must have a performance plan, great leaders must also create a plan to increase and improve professional competencies. Leaders must determine not only goals and a means to grow professionally but also ways to celebrate successful performance. The standards, dispositions, activities, and suggestions provided in *The Courage to Grow* are a start. We challenge you to continue to intentionally grow as a leader. This manual began by reminding you that effective leadership does not happen randomly or by accident. The comprehensive leader is consciously engaged in growth.

Activity 9.1: Celebrating your Performance Growth

Primary goal 1:
Primary goal 2:
Primary goal 3:
Primary goal 4:
Primary goal 5:

Standard/Indicators with Most Significant Growth

1. Number/letter
2.
3.
4.
5.

Exercises/Activities of Greatest Accomplishment

1. Exercise name/activity number
2.
3.
4.
5.

Activity 9.2: Franklin Covey Self-Assessment Seven Habits Profile

Go to the following website: www.franklincovey.com/tc/resources/view/self7. Complete the inventory and chart your results in the lower right quadrant provided for you in the inventory. Share your results with a partner. Which categories were your strengths? Provide examples of times when you demonstrated these categories in your role as a leader.

_____

_____

_____

_____

_____

_____

_____

Activity 9.3: *Encouraging the Heart*, by Kouzes and Posner—Self-Assessment

Place a number next to the statements in table 9.1 that represent you (1 = almost never, 2 = rarely, 3 = seldom, 4 = once in a while, 5 = sometimes, 6 = fairly often, 7 = often, 8 = usually, 9 = very often, and 10 = almost always).

Table 9.1. Self-Assessment

1. ____ I make certain we set a standard that motivates us to do better in the future than we are doing now.

2. ____ I express high expectations about what people are capable of accomplishing.

3. ____ I pay more attention to the positive things people do than to the negative.

4. ____ I personally acknowledge people for their contributions.

5. ____ I tell stories about the special achievements of the members of the team.

6. ____ I make sure that our group celebrates accomplishments together.

7. ____ I get personally involved when we recognize the achievements of others.

8. ____ I clearly communicate my standards to everyone on the team.

9. ____ I let people know that I have confidence in them.

10. ____ I spend a good deal of time listening to the needs and interests of other people.

11. ____ I personalize the recognition I give to another person.

12. ____ I find opportunities to let people know the *why* behind whatever we are doing.

13. ____ I hold special events to celebrate our successes.

14. ____ I show others, by example, how people should be recognized and rewarded.

15. ____ I make it a point to give people feedback on how they are performing against our agreed-upon standards.

16. ____ I express a positive and optimistic outlook even when times are tough.

17. ____ I get to know, at a personal level, the people with whom I work.

18. ____ I find creative ways to make my recognition of others unique and special.

19. ____ I recognize people more in public than in private for their exemplary performance.

20. ____ I find ways to make the workplace enjoyable and fun.

21. ____ I personally congratulate people for a job well done.

____TOTAL (add together all the ratings above; the lowest possible rating you can have is 21, and the highest is 210)

Certificate of Achievement

I, _____,

successfully completed the

exercises and activities with

The Courage to Grow:

Leading with Intentionality!

This is an outstanding

accomplishment, highlighted

by receiving this certificate.

LEADERSHIP TOOLS AND RESOURCES FOR GROWTH

Successories:
www.successories.com

Master Teacher:
www.masterteacher.com

Baudville:
www.baudville.com

Renewal Coaching and Wisdom:
www.wisdomout.com

Leadership Challenge:
www.leadershipchallenge.com

National Blue Ribbon Schools:
www2.ed.gov/programs/nclbbrs/index.html

EPILOGUE

It is predictable that aspiring leaders begin their leadership journey with many questions. Less expected is the fact that, as the experienced leader grows, so do the questions. Could it be that the persistence of questions throughout our role as leaders is an indicator of growth? Is it possible that for the effective leader it is less important to answer all the questions than it is to keep asking them? Are there rhetorical questions that we encourage leaders to ask, such as the following: How can I lead without authority? How can I lead effectively when so many decisions are beyond my control? How can I intentionally channel my passion and desire to grow to make a difference in this world? How will I grow in effectiveness through risk taking and acting with intentionality?

We began this book by asking you to act with intentionality to get ready to develop and change throughout *The Courage to Grow*. Now, as you get to the end of this manual, we encourage you to dialogue with us by contacting us at www.courage-to-lead.com. We would love to hear more about your leadership growth and how you are making a difference. Everything you need is within you.

This manual reminded you that effective leadership does not happen randomly or by accident. The comprehensive leader is consciously engaged in the constant development of knowledge, attitudes, and performance. This leadership growth is conducted with a high level of intention that what is desired can be accomplished. Remember, intention savors moments of peaceful contemplation and productive intuition, and it knows each moment of the day is a precious moment (Radmacher, 2007). Go forth and lead.

REFERENCES

Alimo-Metcalfe, B. (1998). 360-degree feedback and leadership development. *International Journal of Selection and Assessment, 6* (1), 35–44.

Allen, J. B. (2007). *Creating welcoming schools: A practical guide to home-school partnerships with diverse families.* New York: Teachers College Press.

Anderson, M. (1991). *Principals: How to train, recruit, select, induct, and evaluate leaders for America's schools.* Eugene, OR: ERIC Clearinghouse on Educational Management.

Barth, R. (2001). *Learning by heart.* San Francisco: Jossey-Bass.

Blanchard, K. (2010). *Leading at a higher level: Blanchard on leadership and creating high performing organizations.* Upper Saddle River, NJ: FT Press.

Blankenstein, M. (2010). *Failure is not an option: Six principles that guide student achievement in high-performing schools.* Thousand Oaks, CA: Corwin.

Bolles, R. (1995). *What color is your parachute?* New York: Crown.

Burns, J. (1978). *Leadership.* New York: Harper and Row.

Campbell Jones, F., Campbell Jones, B., & Lindsey, R. (2010). *The cultural proficiency journey: Moving beyond ethical barriers toward profound change.* Thousand Oaks, CA: Corwin.

Collaborative for Academic, Social, and Emotional Learning. (n.d.). SEL and academics. Retrieved October 24, 2011, from http://casel.org/why-it-matters/benefits-of-sel/sel-academics.

Council of Chief State School Officers. (2008). *Performance expectations and indicators for education leaders: An ISLLC-based guide to implementing leader standards and a companion guide to the educational leadership policy standards: ISLLC 2008.* Washington, DC: Author.

Covey, S. (2004). *The 8th habit: From effectiveness to greatness.* New York: Free Press.

Danielson, C. (2007). *Enhancing professional practice: A framework for teaching* (2nd ed.). Alexandria, VA: ASCD.

Darling-Hammond, L. (2010). *The flat world of education: How America's commitment to equity will determine our future.* New York: Teachers College Press.

Davis, S. H. (1998). Taking aim at effective leadership. *Thrust for Educational Leadership, 28* (2), 6–12.

Downey, C., Steffy, B., English, F., Frase, L., & Poston, W. (2004). *The three minute walk-through: Changing school supervisory practice one teacher at a time.* Thousand Oaks, CA: Corwin.

DuFour, R., DuFour, R., Eaker, R., & Many, T. (2006). *Learning by doing: A handbook for professional learning communities at work.* Bloomington, IN: Solution Tree.

Dyer, W. (2004). *The power of intention: Learning to co-create your world your way.* Carlsbad, CA: Hay House.

Eaker, R., DuFour, R., & DuFour R. (2002). *Getting started: Reculturing schools to become professional learning communities.* Bloomington, IN: Solution Tree.

Easley, J. (2005). The political tension of education as a public good: The voice of a Martin Luther King, Jr., scholar. *Education and Urban Society, 37,* 490–505.

Elias, M. J., & Arnold, H. (2006). *The educator's guide to emotional intelligence and academic achievement: Social-emotional learning in the classroom.* Thousand Oaks, CA: Corwin.

Epstein, J., Sanders, M., Simon, B., Salinas, K., Jansorn, N., & Voohis, F. (2002). *School, family, and community partnership: Your handbook for action.* Thousand Oaks, CA: Corwin.

Freiburg, K., & Freiburg, J. (1998). *Nuts! Southwest Airlines' crazy recipe for business and personal success.* New York: Crown.

Goodlad, J. (1994). *Educational renewal: Better teachers, better schools.* San Francisco: Jossey-Bass.

Harris, B. M., & Monk, B. J. (1992). *Personnel administration in education* (3rd ed.). Needham Heights, MA: Allyn and Bacon.

Harvey, S., & Goudvis, A. (2000). *Strategies that work: Teaching comprehension to enhance understanding.* Markham, Canada: Stenhouse Publishers.

Hildebrand, V., Phenice, L. A., Gray, M. M., & Hines, R. P. (2007). *Knowing and serving diverse families.* Upper Saddle River, NJ: Prentice Hall.

Illinois Children's Mental Health Partnership. (n.d.). Mission and history. Retrieved October 24, 2011, from http://icmhp.org/aboutus/aboutmission.html.

Illinois State Board of Education. (n.d.). Illinois learning standards: Social/emotional learning (SEL). Retrieved October 24, 2011, from http://www.isbe.net/ils/social_emotional/standards.htm.

Jensen, E. (2009). *Teaching with poverty in mind: What being poor does to kids' brains and what schools can do about it.* Alexandria, VA: ASCD.

Kise, J., & Russell, B. (2007). *Differentiated school leadership: Effective collaboration, communication, and change through personality type.* Thousand Oaks, CA: Corwin.

Kouzes, J., & Posner, B. (2002). *The leadership challenge.* San Francisco: Jossey-Bass.

Kouzes, J., & Posner, B. (2003). *Encouraging the heart: A leader's guide to rewarding and recognizing others.* San Francisco: Jossey-Bass.

Kouzes, J., & Posner, B. (2006). *A leader's legacy.* San Francisco: Jossey-Bass.

Lashway, L. (2003). *Improving principal evaluation.* (ERIC Digest 172, 1–7). Retrieved August 8, 2005, from http://eric.uoregon.edu/publications/digests/digest172.html.

Lepard, D. H. (2002). Using peers and technology to strengthen leadership. *Journal of Personnel Evaluation in Education, 16* (1), 11–28.

Lindsey, D., Jungwirth, L., Pahl, J., & Lindsey, R. (2009). *Culturally proficient learning communities: Confronting inequities through collaborative curiosity.* Thousand Oaks, CA: Corwin.

Lindsey, D., Martinez, R., & Lindsey, R. (2007). *Culturally proficient coaching: Supporting educators to create equitable schools.* Thousand Oaks, CA: Corwin.

Lindsey, R., Robins, K., & Terrell, R. (2003). *Cultural proficiency: A manual for school leaders.* Thousand Oaks, CA: Corwin.

Lundin, S., Christensen, J., Paul, H., & Strand, P. (2002). *Fish! Tales.* New York: Hyperion.

Lyman, L. L., & Villani, C. J. (2004). *Best leadership practices for high-poverty schools.* Lanham, MD: Scarecrow.

Lyubomirsky, S. (2007). *The how of happiness: A scientific approach to getting the life you want.* New York: Penguin.

Marcoux, J., Brown, G., Irby, B., & Lara-Alecio, R. (2003). *A case study on the use of portfolios in principal evaluation.* Paper presented at the Annual Meeting of the American Educational Research. (ERIC ED 475 710)

Marzano, R. J., Waters, T., & McNulty, B. A. (2005). *School leadership that works: From research to results* (1st ed.). Alexandria, VA: ASCD.

Maxwell, J. C. (2001). *The 17 indisputable laws of teamwork: Embrace them and empower your team.* Nashville: Thomas Nelson.

Medina, J. (2008). *Brain rules: 12 principles for surviving and thriving at work, home, and school.* Seattle: Pear Press.

Merrell, K. W., & Gueldner, B. A. 2010. *Social and emotional learning in the classroom: Promoting mental health and academic success.* New York: Guilford.

Mind Tools. (n.d.). Storyboarding: Planning and checking a process as a team. Retrieved October 25, 2011, from http://www.mindtools.com/pages/article/newTMC_77.htm.

National Association for Professional Development Schools. (2008). What it means to be a professional development school. Retrieved June 16, 2011, from www.napds.org/9%20Essentials/statement.pdf.

National Network of Partnership Schools. (1997). Working together for student success. Retrieved June 16, 2011, from www.csos.jhu.edu/p2000.

National Parent Teacher Association. (1990). Family involvement: Building community partnerships (p. 27). Retrieved June 16, 2011, from www.ncrel.org/sdrs/areas/issues/envrnmnt/famncomm/pa4lk16-2.htm.

Nettles, S., & Herrington, C. (2007). Revisiting the importance of the direct effects of school leadership on student achievement: The implications for school improvement policy. *Peabody Journal of Education, 82* (4), 724–36.

Noddings, N. (2005). *The challenge to care in schools: An alternative approach to education.* New York: Teachers College Press.

Parker, G., & Hoffman, R. (2006). *Meeting excellence: 33 tools to lead meetings that get results.* San Francisco: Jossey-Bass.

Patterson, K., Grenny, J., McMillan, R., & Switzler, A. (2002). *Crucial conversations: Tools for talking when stakes are high.* New York: McGraw-Hill.

Pfeffer, J., & Sutton, R. (2000). *The knowing-doing gap: How smart companies turn knowledge into action.* Boston: Harvard Business School.

Pollock, M. 2008. *Everyday Antiracism: Getting Real About Race in School.* New York: New Press.

Radmacher, M. (2007). *Lean forward into your life: Begin each day as if it were on purpose.* San Francisco: Conari Press.

Raelin, J. (2003). *Creating leaderful organizations: How to bring out leadership in everyone.* San Francisco: Berrett-Koehler.

Reeves, D. (2004a). *Assessing educational leaders: Evaluating performance for improved individual and organizational results* (1st ed.). Thousand Oaks, CA: Corwin.

Reeves, D. (2004b). *Accountability in action: A blueprint for learning organizations.* Englewood, CO: Advanced Learning Press.

Reeves, D. (2008). Effective grading practices. Retrieved May 4, 2011, from www.ascd.org/publications/educationalleadership/feb08/vol65/num05/Effective-Grading-Practices.aspx.

Reeves, D. (2009). *Leading change in your school: How to conquer myths, build commitments, and get results.* Alexandria, VA: ASCD.

Reeves, D., & Allison, E. (2009). *Renewal coaching: Sustainable change for individuals and organizations.* San Francisco: Jossey-Bass.

Royea, A., & Appl, D. (2009). Every voice matters: The importance of advocacy. *Early Childhood Education Journal, 37,* 89–91.

Rubin, H. (2002). *Collaborative leadership: Developing effective partnerships in communities and schools.* Thousand Oaks, CA: Corwin.

Sanders, K. (2008). The purposes and practices of leadership assessment as perceived by select public middle and elementary school principals in the Midwest. PhD diss. Aurora University, Aurora, IL.

Secretan, L. H. K. (2004). *Inspire! What great leaders do.* Hoboken, NJ: Wiley.

Sergiovanni, T. (2009). *The principal: A reflective practice perspective.* San Francisco: Pearson.

Servais, K., & Sanders, K. (2006). *The courage to lead: Choosing the road less traveled.* Lanham, MD: Rowman & Littlefield.

Singleton, G., & Linton, C. (2006). *Courageous conversations about race: A field guide for achieving equity in schools.* Thousand Oaks, CA: Corwin.

Sladkey, D. (2009). *Energizing brain breaks: Get refreshed in 1–2 minutes.* Naperville, IL: Energizing Brain Breaks, Inc.

Southern Regional Educational Board. (2010). The three essentials: Improving schools requires district vision, district and state support, and principal leadership. Retrieved October 24, 2011, from www.sreb.org.

Speck, M. (1996, spring). Best practice in professional development for sustained educational change. *ERS Spectrum,* pp. 33–41.

Spring, J. (2005). *Conflict of interests: The politics of American education.* New York: McGraw-Hill.

Strand, P., Christensen, J., & Halper, A. (2006). *Schools of fish: Welcome back to the reason you became an educator.* Burnsville, MN: ChartHouse International Learning Corporation.

Terrell, R, & Lindsey, R. (2008). *Culturally proficient leadership: The personal journey begins within.* Thousand Oaks, CA: Corwin.

Thomas, D. W., Holdaway, E. A., & Ward, K. L. (2000). Policies and practices involved in the evaluation of school principals. *Journal of Personnel Evaluation in Education, 14* (3), 215–40.

Valentine, J. W. (2005). The Instructional Practices Inventory: A process for profiling student engaged learning for school improvement. Retrieved August 18, 2011, from http://education.missouri.edu/orgs/mllc/Upload%20Area-Docs/IPI%20Manuscript%208-05.pdf.

Weaver-Hart, A. (1994). *Evaluating principals in light of context and socialization.* Paper presented at the American Educational Research Association. (ERIC ED 380 879)

White, D. R., Crooks, S. M., & Melton, J. K. (2002). Design dynamics of a leadership assessment academy: Principal self-assessment using research and technology. *Journal of Personnel Evaluation in Education, 16* (1), 45–61.

Wilmore, E. (2002). *Principal leadership: Applying the new educational leadership constituent council (ELCC) standards.* Thousand Oaks, CA: Corwin.

York-Barr, J., Sommers, A., Ghere, G., & Montie, J. (2001). *Reflective practice to improve schools: An action guide for educators.* Thousand Oaks, CA: Corwin.

Zajda, J. (2009). *Globalization, education, and social justice.* New York: Springer.

INDEX

ABOUT THE AUTHORS

Kristine Servais has been a middle school and elementary teacher, middle school assistant principal and principal, and director of field experiences for pre-service teachers, and is presently associate professor of educational leadership. The middle school at which she was principal was recognized as a National Blue Ribbon School of Excellence. Kristine has studied school principals and, in particular, transformational leadership as a means for schools to collaboratively create a community of learners. Her dissertation focused on the roles, responsibilities, and relationships of the principal as a transformational leader in school-university partnerships. Kristine provides administrator workshops and academies on the topics of professional learning communities, meeting management, team building, and type preference.

Kellie Sanders was a middle school teacher for ten years and a middle school assistant principal. Kellie has been an elementary principal in several districts for the past ten years. She has her master's degree and doctorate in educational administration, and her primary focus has been on the purpose, perceptions, and practices of leadership assessment. Kellie has co-written an article along with Mary Lynne Derrington in the *AASA Journal of Scholarship and Practice* titled "Conceptualizing a System for Principal Evaluation." An area of continued focus for Kellie has been facilitating professional development for teachers and principals in the areas of diversity, equity, social justice, and social-emotional learning.

Made in the USA
Lexington, KY
06 January 2014